Moments
of Decision

Moments
of Decision

Guidelines for
the Most Important Choices
of Your Life

Vance Havner

BAKER BOOK HOUSE
Grand Rapids, Michigan 49506

Unless otherwise identified, Scripture quotations in this volume are from the King James Version of the Bible.

Scripture quotations identified PHILLIPS are from THE NEW TESTAMENT IN MODERN ENGLISH (Revised Edition), translated by J. B. Phillips. © J. B. Phillips 1958, 1960, 1972. Used by permission of Macmillan Publishing Co., Inc

Contents

Preface

Once to every man and nation
Comes the moment to decide,
In the strife of truth with falsehood,
For the good or evil side.
JAMES RUSSELL LOWELL

History is a record of decisions, good and bad. Our lives are the sum total of our decisions and their consequences. Character is the finished product of our choices, crystallized, set, hardened into a pattern. The day comes when Revelation 22:11 applies: "He that is unjust, let him be unjust still: and he which is filthy, let him be filthy still: and he that is righteous, let him be righteous still: and he that is holy, let him be holy still."

History is made by men of decision, good and bad. Someone asked an old servant of Andrew Jackson: "Do you think General Jackson will go to heaven?" "I don't know," was the reply, "but if he made up his mind to go, he did!" This world is not moved by double-minded men, unstable in all their ways.

The Bible is a record of great decisions, good and bad. It begins with the worst choice of all when Eve listened to the devil and decided to eat of the forbidden fruit. All the sin of humanity down the centuries since Eve is the fruit of that fatal decision. But God so loved the world that He gave His Son, and that Suffering Servant set His face like a flint and chose the way of Calvary. Our Lord did not have a hard face, but He had a set face. He stead-

7

fastly set His face to go to Jerusalem. His mind was made up; He was going somewhere. The world is full of sin today. It was a devilish decision that provided the cause. It was a *divine* decision that provides the cure. One decision remains: we must accept the provision. God has invested every man with the awful responsibility of choice. We cannot change our hearts, but we can change our minds; and when we change our minds, God will change our hearts. "He that believeth on him is not condemned: but he that believeth not is condemned already, because he hath not believed in the name of the only begotten Son of God" (John 3:18). That is life's greatest decision. Everyone who has reached accountability has already made that decision for or against. Not to be for Jesus Christ is to be against Him. "He that is not with me is against me; and he that gathereth not with me scattereth abroad" (Matthew 12:30). That statement admits only two kinds of people; there is no middle ground, no third class. But while life lasts, we can change from lost to saved, from scattering to gathering, from sinner to saint.

The Bible is a book of great decisions, and from start to finish it calls us to the greatest decision of all. It lists many other choices, and we shall look at some of them in the hope that we may be warned by the defeat of some men and encouraged by the victory of others.

Moments
of Decision

1 Abraham's Decision

The First Pilgrim Father

Abraham was a *patriarch.* He was not only the father of the Jewish nation but the father of the faithful. He was the progenitor of all who walk by faith and not by sight. He was a *priest* setting up an altar wherever he went. Every Christian is a priest, not offering a sacrifice for sins—since that has been done once and for all—but offering his person, praise, and possessions.

Abraham was a *pilgrim.* When I titled this The First Pilgrim Father, I thought I had something original, only to discover that F. B. Meyer used the term years ago! (Which reminds me of an old evangelist who said, "When I started out preaching, I said I'd be original or nothing—and soon found out I was both!")

Abraham is the first and an outstanding example of the believer who, as an exile and alien in this world, is called a stranger and sojourner. God's people are not citizens of earth trying to get to heaven but citizens of heaven trying to get through this world. Trying to get this across to the average Sunday-morning congregation of American church members is almost hopeless for no generation has ever driven down its tent pegs in this world as we have done. This wonderland of plastics and gadgets, of deep freezers and giveaway shows, of ranch houses in suburbia and push-button living seems good

11

enough for most of the saints today. Bunyan's immortal
Christian had no use for Vanity Fair, his clothes, conver-
sation, and conduct were out of place. Nowadays, he
cannot be distinguished from the worldlings.

Dr. J. B. Phillips says of the early Christians:

> . . . To these men this world was only a part, and
> because of the cumulative result of human sin a
> highly infected and infectious part, of God's vast
> created universe, seen and unseen. They trained
> themselves therefore and attempted to train others,
> not to be "taken in" by this world, nor to give their
> hearts to it, nor to conform to its values, but to re-
> member constantly that they were only temporary
> residents, and that their rights of citizenship were in
> the unseen world of Reality. . . . as we read what
> they have to say we may perhaps find ourselves say-
> ing a little wistfully, "perhaps these men were
> right".
>
> Preface, Letters to Young Churches

Read that paragraph to the average American Christian, and you will get only a vacant stare. When have you
heard a congregation sing "In the Sweet By and By"?
Settled as comfortably as we are with credit cards and
Social Security, who is interested in being bound for the
Promised Land? We have exchanged pie in the sky for
retirement benefits and have feathered our nests so well
that we have no desire to fly.

Then, too, the church has gone into social reform with
a vengeance, and Vanity Fair is being done over in a vast
urban-renewal project of glorified socialism under religious auspices. All this plays havoc with New Testament
Pilgrim Christianity.

We once believed, with Matthew Henry, that this
world is our passage and not our portion. We used to feel

like traveling on; now we feel like settling down. The Scriptures warn us against the love of money, the cares of this life, and the pride of it. We are bidden to love not the world but to lay up treasure in heaven (see Matthew 6:20). The Bible reminds us that a man's life consists not in the abundance of his possessions (*see* Luke 12:15), and admonishes us to be content with the food, raiment, and things such as we have. Of course God's people have a right to the common comforts of life. There is no holiness in a hair shirt, but the new fad of equating Christianity with earthly prosperity is hard put to it to find New Testament texts to justify its position. Our Saviour had nowhere to lay His head. He was not at home down here. The early saints bear little resemblance to the new variety who are out not to overcome the world but to enjoy it. The heroes of faith in Hebrews 11 do not remind us of modern, *successful* Christians. And what shall we say of the apostles who were virtually the world's rubbish, the scum of the earth? The inspiration of most Christians today is not the cross-bearing disciple but the popular big shot. Something happened when Constantine paganized Christianity while trying to Christianize paganism. We lost our pilgrim character and the marks of our heavenly citizenship. We settled like Lot in Sodom, and the church became another gigantic supercorporation. It was a dark day when we forgot that we have no home down here.

It is possible to have a big bank account and be poor in spirit, but the combination is rare. Smyrnan piety is not often mixed with Laodicean prosperity. When we are rich and increased with goods, we usually have need of nothing. We Christians are transients in this world, not residents. We are spiritual children of Abraham, not sons of Lot.

God said first to Abraham, *get out.* "Now the Lord had

said unto [Abraham], Get thee out of thy country, and
from thy kindred, and from thy father's house, unto a
land that I will shew thee" (Genesis 12:1). Terah, Abraham's father, had started toward Canaan but got only as
far as Haran and died there. That is about as far as many
would-be pilgrims get. Our Lord spoke of hating father,
mother, wife, children, brethren, and sisters, of letting
the dead bury their dead, and of forsaking all to follow
Him (*see* Luke 14:26). It is not enough to sing "The Way
of the Cross Leads Home" if we are not ready to include
the last verse:

> Then I bid farewell to the way of the world,
> To walk in it nevermore.

Pilgrim Christians must renounce this world setup,
which is no friend of the grace that helps us on to God.
When prospects show up for church membership these
days, nothing is said about telling the world good-bye. It
is said that they will grow out of all that, as we instruct
them, but most of them do not; so we have a flock of
worldlings, who are not about to give up their idols.
Abraham did not argue or debate the issue. I read, "So
Abraham departed, as the Lord had spoken unto
him . . ." (Genesis 12:4). "By faith Abraham . . .
obeyed . . ." (Hebrews 11:8). *He got out.*

God's *pilgrim* must not only *get out,* he must *go on.*
We read that Abraham departed, went forth, passed
through, removed. He went out, not knowing whither he
went. A preacher friend told me that his grandfather
used to take him on short trips when he was a little boy.
One day when Grandfather asked him to go along, the
boy asked, "Where are you going?" Grandfather went on
without him and when the boy asked later, "Why did

you not take me?" he was told, "Because you asked,
'Where are you going?' If you had really wanted to go
with me, it wouldn't have mattered where I was going."
The pilgrim does not ask God, "Where are you taking
me?"

> Anywhere with Jesus I can safely go,
> Anywhere He leads me in this world below.
> JESSIE B. POUNDS

God does not furnish us with a detailed road map. A
traveler in Africa complained to his guide, "There is no
road, no path, in this jungle. We have lost our way." The
guide replied, "There is no way; *I am the way*." Our
Lord is the *Way;* when we are with Him, we may not
know *whither* but we know *whom*.

Our pilgrimage is not a vacation but a vocation. It is
not a pleasure trip. There are joys on the way, but there
are solemn and serious responsibilities. Abraham found
that to be true with regard to Ishmael and Isaac. Ishmael,
born outside the will of God, born of the flesh, was the
worst thing in Abraham's life. God took Ishmael away,
and he never came back. Isaac, born in the will of God,
born of faith, was the best thing in Abraham's life. God
took Isaac, but gave him back. God wants both the
Ishmaels and Isaacs in our lives, and we must lay the
dearest on His altar. Abraham also had to separate from
Lot. When we begin our pilgrimage, we are not only
called upon to get out of the world, but we may have to
separate from some Christians on our pilgrimage. On the
other hand, Abraham rescued Lot when he was taken
captive. It is the separated man who can help weaker
Christians, in time of trouble.

Abraham made mistakes, of course. He told a half-
truth about Sarai when he detoured to Egypt during a

famine. In emergencies, we often forget God and fall
back on our own wits, but a half-truth is also a half-lie.
Anything told with intent to deceive is always a costly
mistake and a sin in the sight of God.

The general tenor of Abraham's life was faith and
faithfulness. We read that "He staggered not at the promise of God through unbelief; but was strong in faith, giving glory to God" (Romans 4:20). Some are saved from
sin, but not from staggering! James tells us to pray in
faith, nothing wavering. If we are to *get on* in our jour-
ney, we must walk without wobbling.

Finally, as pilgrims, we are concerned not only with
getting out and *getting on* but *getting home*. Abraham
was not sure of his earthly destination, but he was interested most in his heavenly destination. "For he
looked for a city which hath foundations, whose builder
and maker is God" (Hebrews 11:10). We read in Hebrews 11 that all these pilgrims died in faith, strangers
and pilgrims in the earth, seeking a country, desiring a
heavenly country. God is not ashamed to be called their
God, for He hath prepared for them a city. I do not hear
many sermons on heaven these days. The average
church member has a very nebulous idea of that pearly
white city if indeed he has any at all. Heaven and hell
have become bywords. In the hour of death or bereave-
ment, there may be a fleeting interest in the hereafter.
Strangely enough, there is demonic deception aplenty
on the subject, and multitudes are going after witches
and sorcerers and fortune-tellers and ESP and seances
and hallucinations and every form of hocus-pocus under
the sun relating to a life beyond. I hear little about the
old-fashioned homesickness for heaven that made the
saints sing "When I Can Read My Title Clear to Man-
sions in the Skies" or:

My latest sun is sinking fast,
My race is nearly run . . .
Come, come, Angel Band
Come, and around me stand,
Bear me away on your snowy wings
To my eternal home.

Of course every child of God is going home, but there ought to be a zest and a thrill about it. We ought to make that last lap to home base the best run of the game. When I was a boy on a farm, our old horse, after the day's work was done, climbed the hill up to our house at a clip that belied how tired he was. He was going home! If an old farm horse can end the day like that, we saints of God ought to sing with fervor, "One sweetly solemn thought comes to me o'er and o'er, I'm nearer to my heavenly home than I have been before." Today, worldliness has become mere secularism. The social gospelers are so obsessed with this-worldliness that *un*worldliness and *other*-worldliness are laughed at, and *next*-worldliness is rated low. It is as though it were sinful to talk about going to heaven, when our present business is to build heaven on earth. There are two cities in Revelation: Babylon and the New Jerusalem. Too many dear souls are mixed up and so busy building Babylon, readying the world church-world state for Antichrist, that they have no civic pride in the city that is to come down from God out of heaven.

Thank God, there is still a band of us pilgrims who have *gotten out,* who are *going on,* and who are happy to be *getting home.* We are the children of Abraham, the first of the pilgrim fathers, but we do not have to wait to get home to begin our celestial enjoyment.

> The hill of Zion yields
> A thousand sacred sweets
> Before we reach the heavenly fields
> Or walk the golden streets.
>
> ISAAC WATTS

The trees of that fair land bend over the wall, and we sample some of the fruit in advance. Our blessed assurance is a foretaste of glory divine. The Spirit within us is the earnest of our inheritance. The sample has whetted our appetite and we quicken our pace, for:

> Then we shall be where we would be;
> Then we shall be what we should be;
> Things that are not now, nor could be,
> Soon shall be our own.

2 Lot's Decision

Settled in Sodom

"Likewise also as it was in the days of Lot; they did eat, they drank, they bought, they sold, they planted, they builded; But the same day that Lot went out of Sodom it rained fire and brimstone from heaven, and destroyed them all. Even thus shall it be in the day when the Son of man is revealed" (Luke 17:28–30). It shall not be as in the days of Solomon, but as in the days of Sodom. Solomon's day was a time of peace, progress, and prosperity; Sodom is a synonym for the lowest, filthiest, and vilest in human degradation. Sodom was a moral cancer and God cauterized it, burned it out. No account of divine judgment is mentioned more in the Bible. We read about it in Deuteronomy, Isaiah, Jeremiah, Lamentations, Ezekiel, Amos, Zephaniah, Second Peter, Jude, and Revelation as well as in Matthew and Luke.

The condition of Sodom is analyzed in Ezekiel 16:49: "Behold, this was the iniquity of thy sister Sodom, pride, fulness of bread, and abundance of idleness . . . ." These are the marks of our time. We have never been so proud of ourselves as now; we never had less reason to be. Man has made himself the center of the universe. He used to stand on a starry night and say with the Psalmist, "When I consider thy heavens, the work of thy fingers, the moon and the stars, which thou hast ordained; *What is man*, that thou art mindful of him? and the son of man, that thou visitest him?" (Psalms 8:3, 4, italics mine). Now we contemplate man and cynically say, "What are the moon and stars?" I have read that Theodore Roosevelt took a visitor to his home at Sagamore Hill out on the front lawn, one night, to survey the skies. After a while, the Colonel said, "Now I think we are down to our right size, let's go back indoors."

Today we try to mount up to the stars scientifically, but meanwhile we sink into the slime morally. Our minds are in space but our souls are in Sodom. We have conquered the atom, but we have not mastered Adam. We still live in a world under the dominion of Satan—and it was pride that threw him out of heaven to begin with.

There is also *fulness of bread* in our modern Sodom. As in the days of Lot, so it is in America. Our technology and know-how have produced a surplus of food and commodities. When I was a boy, all that one needed to be a farmer was a plow, a mule, and a few acres of ground. Today a farmer must have a college degree and be an expert while the government pays him *not* to farm. On one hand, we study how to step up production and, on the other, how to slow it down. All this can be explained in Washington, of course, but there is a better answer: As it was in the days of Lot.

Along with fulness of bread goes *abundance of idleness*. This well-fed generation of Americans with forty million of us overweight (I suppose you'd call that round figures), has time on its hands. Overproduction brings idleness, and man does not know what to do with his spare time. That is evident from the way he spends it! Automation has brought us leisure, and with our heads and hands far ahead of our hearts, some are beginning to wonder what will happen to the soul of man. Some time ago a booklet was issued on "How to Do Nothing in a Constructive Manner"! The Bible says "Six days shalt thou labour, and do all thy work" (Exodus 20:9), and we fare badly when we tamper with that arrangement. We have never had more to live *on* and less to live *for*. Work is God's provision to keep us out of meanness. Much of the youthful unrest today is due to the fact that too many youngsters never do a day's work.

Sodomy is a synonym for homosexuality and today we have more Sodomites than in all history. It is part of the new morality that makes illegitimacy respectable and subsidizes it in the welfare state. I am not surprised that Sodom was destroyed by fire and brimstone from heaven. It was peculiar fire and the Scriptures indicate that the heavens and earth are kept in store reserved unto fire against the day when the elements shall melt with fervent heat and the earth and its works be burned up. (*See* 2 Peter 3:10–12.) This takes on new meaning in this nuclear age when atomic destruction looms over us every day. How timely that word, *as it was in the days of Lot*.

We are all caught in the middle of modern Sodom and here is where Lot comes in. He was a perfect example of what *not* to do about Sodom. His eyes beheld the fertile plain of Jordan. He saw a chance to get rich quick. *"Then Lot chose him all the plain of Jordan . . ."* (Genesis 13:11). [Italics mine.] That was his fateful decision, his monumental blunder. Lot did not take moral and spiritual dangers into consideration. He pitched his tent toward Sodom. (*See* Genesis 13:12.) When a man pitches his tent toward Sodom, give him a little more time and he will be in the middle of Sodom. Lot became an alderman, he sat in the gate, he was president of the Whatsits and secretary of the Whoozits, and he may have said, "If Abraham wants to live in tents, let him do it; I've got it made." But he lost his influence with his family—seeming as one that mocked, to his sons-in-law—and died in disgrace with his own daughters.

A man never makes a bigger fool of himself than when he settles down in Sodom for personal advantage. I would never had known that Lot was a righteous man but for the New Testament. Peter tells us that his righteous soul was vexed with the unlawful deeds of his neighbors. (*See* 2 Peter 2:6–8.) But that is not enough, he had no business settling down with that crowd for selfish gain at the expense of his soul.

Geographically, we have to live in the Sodom of this age. Paul says that if we do not keep company with the fornicators and covetous and extortioners and idolaters, we would have to leave the world (*see* 1 Corinthians 5:9, 10); but we can be *in* it and not *of* it. As it was in the days of Lot, so it is today, and too many Christians live like Lot in Sodom instead of being pilgrims with Abraham. We live in a world order as rotten as Sodom ever was. Civilization is doomed to judgment. I do not say it has gone to the dogs—out of respect for dogs! We are not here to save civilization. God is calling out a people for His Name. Lot did not reform Sodom but Sodom ruined Lot!

It was a matter of choice and he made the wrong decision. Abraham let God choose his inheritance for him. The greatest choice any man makes is to let God choose for him. It is still a decision but it is a decision to let God decide. Lot did his own choosing and it ended in his collapse. That kind of decision always ends in disaster.

Too many prominent church members are aldermen in Sodom. Too many professing Christians have pitched their tents toward Sodom. The lust of the flesh, the lust of the eyes, the pride of life, that is Sodom. The Living Bible puts it this way: ". . . the craze for sex, the ambition to buy everything that appeals to you, and the pride that comes from wealth and importance—these are not from God. They are from this evil world itself" (1 John 2:16). That is Sodom today, American Sodom with its pride, its fulness of bread, and abundance of idleness. And as it was in the days of Lot, so shall it be, and so it is.

You will observe that Abraham let Lot make his choice. Then God said to Abraham, "Now look in all directions, it's all yours." (*See* Genesis 13:14.) The man who walks with God can afford to let the man of this world take his choice. The meek shall inherit the earth and the saints shall judge it. So everything will be ours eventually anyway. What the millionaires of this age do not know is that they are only renters. The title deeds belong to the saints who walk by faith with Abraham and not by sight with Lot. Then God said to Abraham, "I am thy exceeding great reward." (*See* Genesis 15:1.) God is our Rewarder but, better than that, He is our Reward. Some never see any farther than God as their Rewarder. He is a Rewarder but too many make a Santa Claus out of the Lord. Blessed is the man who can honestly sing:

> Once earthly joy I craved,
> Sought peace and rest;
> *Now Thee alone* I seek,
> Give what is best. . . .
> **ELIZABETH PRENTISS**

When a man gets to that altitude, he is above disappointment for, come what may, he still has God and, having God, he has everything. That is what you get, when you choose God. When you choose Sodom, that is all you get, you have your reward.

3 Moses' Decision

"Choosing . . . Affliction With the People of God"

The New Testament biography of Moses is a thumbnail sketch in the Epistle to the Hebrews. It begins, as every biography should, with the family background on a note of *parental courage:* "By faith Moses, when he was born, was hid three months of his parents, because they saw he was a proper child; and they were not afraid of the king's commandment" (Hebrews 11:23). Not fearing the king's commandment paid off, for when Moses grew up, he feared not the wrath of the king. Like parents, like children!

Egypt is a type of this world; its Pharaoh is the devil, the prince of darkness. Any God-fearing parent, who tries to bring up children in this world order today, knows what it means to buck the edicts of Pharaoh in style, popularity, or earthly success. To rear children in the nurture and admonition of the Lord nowadays calls for all the wisdom the parents of any teenager can pray down from heaven. Just as with Moses, the devil today is out to destroy every promising child, but when a godly mother and Almighty God are in partnership, old Pharaoh does not have a chance. It takes a lot of Chris-

24

tian courage not to fear the commandments of Pharaoh and risk being called unconventional and uncooperative in suburbia, where there might be only one dedicated family in the block.

Amidst all the hand wringing over juvenile delinquency, we forget that too many church-member parents would rather have their children succeed and be popular in Egypt than bound for the Promised Land. Then too, there is a wholesale surrender to the mood of the age and the trend of the times. I know Christian parents who have lowered their standards and compromised their convictions to please their children; thus while the children are growing up, the parents are growing down. This adult generation lacks the backbone, grit, and courage to take an unpopular stand against Pharaoh. There are some wonderful exceptions, but the exceptions prove the rule. This same surrender is going on in the schools, the churches, and the government. Youth has been put on the pedestal, and one might well say with the preacher in Ecclesiastes 10:16: "Woe to thee, O land, when thy king is a child . . . ." Isaiah bemoaned the day when children should be princes and babes rule over the people, when the child should behave proudly against the ancient (*see* Isaiah 3:4, 5).

Family background is not enough. Ancestry is often like potatoes, the best part is under the ground. A boy must make his own decision; so Moses came to *a personal choice.* It was a double choice, both negative and positive. It was negative in that he refused to be called the son of Pharaoh's daughter; he turned down the pleasures of sin for a season; he renounced the treasures of Egypt and forsook Egypt itself. It was positive in that he chose to suffer affliction with the people of God and esteemed the reproach of Christ greater riches than the treasures of Egypt. (*See* Hebrews 11:26.)

Consider what a choice this young man made. He was
the only free Hebrew of his time. His prospects were
brilliant; wealth, ease, refinement, pleasure, and power
were at his fingertips. Josephus says Moses was in line
for the throne of Egypt, one of the greatest civilizations
of all time. All this the adopted son of Pharaoh's daughter could have had, yet he cast his lot with a nation of
slaves. He chose to risk his life for a host of ignorant
bondmen living in exile. They were a weak, vacillating
multitude of undisciplined servants, easily discouraged,
often rebellious, and quick to fall into the sinful ways of
the heathen. They vexed Moses, until he lost his pa-
tience, spoke unadvisedly with his lips, and missed getting into the Promised Land himself. Nine out of ten
would call him a fool for making such a choice, but he
was right.

He was right in his refusal. A man must say no to some
things if he is to live for God. Nehemiah wrote, "So did
not I, because of the fear of God" (*see* Nehemiah 5:15).
[Italics, mine.] A righteous man walks *not* in the counsel
of the ungodly, stands *not* in the way of sinners, sits *not*
in the seat of the scornful. (*See* Psalms 1:1.) If we are to
travel the way of the cross, we must say good-bye to the
way of the world, to walk in it nevermore. The vain
things that charm us most we must sacrifice to His blood.
We live in a day when it is more and more difficult to say
no. We work both sides of the street—run with the hare
and hunt with the hounds. We are in church on Sunday
morning with Moses; all week we are in Egypt with
Pharaoh. We would have the most of both worlds. We
would like to work out an arrangement by which we
might dwell in the Promised Land and also keep our old
connections back in Egypt. Our church rolls are filled
with a motley mob, stranded in the wilderness, longing
for the fleshpots of the old life, preferring a taste of garlic

to a foretaste of glory. Christians need to be called back to the great renunciation: "Then said Jesus unto his disciples, If any man will come after me, let him deny himself, and take up his cross, and follow me" (Matthew 16:24).

Moses was right, not only in what he refused, but in what he chose—choosing rather to suffer affliction with the people of God and the reproach of Christ. This is a foreign language to the average church-goer today. We leave comfortable homes to ride in comfortable cars to sit in comfortable churches to hear comfortable sermons. What do we know about the reproach of Christ? We sing:

> To the old rugged cross I will ever be true,
> Its shame and reproach gladly bear.
>   GEORGE BENNARD

Then we fold up the reproach in the hymnbook and go out with not the faintest notion of what we have been singing about. We read, "Let us go forth therefore unto him without the camp, bearing his reproach" (Hebrews 13:13), but what are the afflictions of the people of God and what is the reproach of Christ? They certainly are not the ordinary kind of troubles to which everyone is heir. We are not bearing our crosses every time we have a headache; an aspirin tablet will take care of that. What is meant is the trouble we would not have if we were not Christians, the trouble we do have because of our identification with Jesus Christ in His death and Resurrection. We do not hear much about cross bearing these days. Some people would never join church if they thought it would cost anything to be a Christian; so now we emphasize how much fun one can have in a deluxe country-club Christianity. The former pastor of the church where I belong says that less than a hundred years ago the members of the church were ridiculed and the pastor was hissed as he walked along the street. Things are different now and it is not because times are better. We are a weaker breed of Christians, who know little of the scandal of the cross. A dedicated New Testament Christian will suffer scorn and opposition, will be an odd number, a stranger in the eyes of this godless generation, for all who will live godly in Christ Jesus shall suffer persecution. (*See* 2 Timothy 3:12.)

We read that Moses esteemed the reproach of Christ greater riches than the treasures in Egypt. He made a survey, took stock, added up all the facts on both sides, and made his decision. He looked at Egypt's best and Israel's worst; he cast his lot with the people of God. Furthermore he had respect unto the recompense of the reward. (*See* Hebrews 11:26.) He looked into the future and saw not a nation of slaves, but the kingdom that was to be under David and Solomon and that greater kingdom where Christ would reign over a redeemed Israel. When we choose our crowd, we should do it with the long view. God's people are not much to look at now, but their day is coming. They suffer now and reign later; they bear the cross now and wear the crown hereafter. You do not hear much about that in modern Christianity, but it is New Testament Christianity; Moses saw it through the telescope of faith in his day. His contemporaries may have said, "That Hebrew is crazy," but here I am, centuries later, writing about Moses. He lost his life to save it; he went down to go up. He staked his fortunes on eternity instead of Egypt, and he won.

Moses made his greatest decision as a young man. We commonly think that life's major decisions are made by older people, but, actually, the three greatest choices anyone can make are usually decided upon by young people before they reach their middle twenties. The salvation of the soul, the choice of a life work and a life companion, these are life's greatest decisions, and *young* people make them. When one makes that first choice and trusts Christ, it is all-inclusive: all other decisions are wrapped up in it.

Moses could have said: "I don't want to get involved with a crowd of slaves. I've got a chance to grow up in Pharaoh's court." He could have played it safe like the Reubenites who did not fight with Deborah and Barak, but preferred the shepherd's flutes at home to the bugle call to battle. Moses could have played it cool; however he would have missed being a leader in one of history's greatest dramas. He dared to take a lonely stand. Too many of us are like noodles. Noodles have to be mixed with soup or meat or something else. Nobody sits down to a bowl of plain noodles. Some Christians have to be mixed with something else; they cannot stand alone. I would certainly hate to be a noodle!

Moses chose the reproach of *Christ*. At the heart of his devotion was a Person. People get involved these days in causes and movements, even in Christianity, but not with Christ. We live in an impersonal age, and man has become as impersonal as the machines he operates. Even religious activity becomes a cold program of projects; it lacks the warmth of a Person. Preaching lacks the fire of the Holy Spirit, who is a Person. Of course there must be involvement with people. Our Lord identified Himself with sinful mankind; however our involvement with people should grow out of our identification with Him. Too many, who have never become personally involved with Christ Himself, are trying to change society and make the world over.

Then, Moses chose the *reproach* of Christ. We need to recover the scandal of our faith. We are doing everything under the sun to remove the shame of the cross and to make the Gospel popular. Everything is pitched in a different key today. The cross has become a pretty charm to wear around the neck. We preach a new Christianity that stresses similarities, not contrasts; that parallels the world instead of intersecting it; that makes no unpleasant demands of its converts. It imitates everything the world offers and copies, instead of contradicts, the spirit of the age. Christianity is just a better way to have a good time. We would make it acceptable to a generation that cannot endure sound doctrine and wants its itching ears tickled.

Finally, Moses esteemed the reproach of Christ greater *riches* than the treasures in Egypt. *Reproach* and *riches*—who ever thought of finding riches in reproach? The wealthiest man is he who has suffered most for Christ. Today many wear medals, but few wear scars. If you have no wounds to show, you probably have not been in many battles, only to dress parades on Sunday! Paul said he bore in his body the marks of the Lord Jesus. He listed his scars, stripes, prisons, beatings, stonings, shipwrecks, perils, weariness, painfulness, watchings, hunger, thirst, fastings, cold, and nakedness. (*See* 2 Corinthians 11:23–27.) We many not bear the marks of physical suffering, but we ought to show evidence of our identification with our Lord in His death and Resurrection. Thomas wanted to see the marks of the cross. The world is looking, not for our medals, but for our scars. The richest Christian is the one most marked by the reproach of Christ, which is greater wealth than the treasures in Egypt.

Moses' life was marked not only by *parental courage* and *personal choice* but by *persevering continuance.* He endured as seeing Him who is invisible. (*See* Hebrews 11:27.) We read that when he first tried to deliver Israel, he looked this way and that way. (*See* Exodus 2:12.) He was cross-eyed and nobody ever accomplished much for

God by looking two ways. He tried to kill the Egyptians
on the retail plan, one at a time, but after his post-
graduate course in Midian he looked only one way; having chosen the imperishable, he saw the invisible and
did the impossible. Moses made his choice and so must
we. He said no to Egypt and yes to God. He chose the
afflictions of the people of God instead of the pleasures
of sin for a season. We cannot have both.

We have developed a *neither–nor* Christianity, neither
fish nor fowl. In World War I, Theodore Roosevelt spoke
of German-Americans with divided loyalty as hyphen-
ated Americans. He said, "If you are an American and
something else, you are not an American." He reminded
us that America is not a "polyglot boardinghouse." The
kingdom of God is not a polyglot boardinghouse either.
If you are a Christian and something else, you are not a
Christian. No man can serve two masters. (*See* Matthew
6:24.) We need a new breed of Christians who are
willing to be called the scum of the earth and a spectacle
to the world for the scandal of the cross.

4   Joshua's Decision

"As for Me and My House"

Almost two hundred years ago a redheaded Virginian stood in an old church in Richmond and made a speech that helped to turn the tide of history. He was tired of finagling with George III. He was tired of the olive-branch men and peaceful coexistence. He reached his climax when he declared, "I know not what course others may take *but as for me*, give me liberty or give me death!" [Italics, mine.] No applause followed that speech. The effect was too profound. The grandfather of Robert E. Lee arose and supported it. One man expressed a desire to be buried on that spot when he died—and he was. Patrick Henry had made a great decision. America is the product of great decisions.

Today some laugh at old-fashioned oratory, but when one considers most of the speeches we hear nowadays, it is a poor time to ridicule Patrick Henry. On the other hand, long-haired radicals try to use the American Revolution to justify their Communist-inspired anarchy. The words of the redheaded Virginian will be remembered as long as freedom endures. Patrick Henry made a momentous choice when he said, *"but as for me . . . ."*

Centuries ago Joshua made a great speech to the children of Israel. Near the close of his life he gathered the

32

people for a farewell message. It has all the marks of a
revival sermon. He began with a rundown of past blessings. He called upon Israel to renounce their idols and
serve God. It was negative and positive, both barrels of
the gun. Then he gave the invitation to action: "Choose
ye this day whom ye will serve" and climaxed it with his
own decision, "*As for me* and my house, we will serve
the Lord." (*See* Joshua 24:15.)

It was high time for a decision. The Israelites were in
the Promised Land, but they had not driven out their
enemies as God had commanded. They were trying to
live in peaceful coexistence, peace without victory.
Whether with Canaanites then or Communists now, it
cannot be done. Douglas MacArthur made that clear
when he said, "There is no substitute for victory."

Joshua knew the weakness of Israel. Abraham had
been called out of idolatry, and the seeds of evil
lay dormant ready to spring into weeds of apostasy.
He remembered how at Sinai they had promised
to serve God, only to worship a golden calf six weeks
later.

The church today would live at peaceful coexistence
with the world, the flesh, and the devil. There is as much
idolatry among us as there ever was in Israel. The love of
money, of sensual pleasure, of ourselves—these evils
beset us as never before. John's last word in his First
Epistle was, "Little children, keep yourselves from
idols." . . . Revival comes when we pray:

Lord Jesus, I long to be perfectly whole;
I want Thee forever to live in my soul,
Break down every idol, cast out every foe;
Now wash me and I shall be whiter than snow.
                              JAMES NICHOLSON

Charles Finney said: "Revival is a new beginning of
obedience to God." It means a decision to renounce
idols and serve God. It is personal. *"But as for me. . . ."*

Paul wrote to Timothy in his first letter, chapter 6
about the peril of *things*, of the *times*, and concerning
the *truth*. Each time he followed it with the injunction
but as for you, as some new translations put it. "The love
of money is the root of all evil *but as for you* [Italics,
mine], flee these things." "Perilous times shall come *but
as for you*, continue in the things you have learned";
"The time will come when they cannot endure sound
doctrine *but as for you*, watch in all things, endure afflictions, do the work of an evangelist, make full proof of thy
ministry." We must decide about *things*, about the *times*,
and about the *truth*.

The people responded to Joshua's challenge declaring
that they too would serve the Lord, but it wa not an
enduring revival. As we move from Joshua into Judges,
we see that the misery in the Book of Judges is due to the
mistakes recorded in the Book of Joshua. The last verse
in Judges reads, "In those days there was no king in
Israel: every man did that which was right in his own
eyes." When there is coexistence with evil, false peace
without victory, superficial religion, we are on the way to
lawlessness. Authority goes out and anarchy comes in.
There is no king in Israel and every man does what is
right in his own eyes. We have arrived at this point today
with civil disobedience, contextual morality, situation
ethics and anarchy.

When the congregation vowed thei resolve to follow
Joshua's decision, he replied, "Ye cannot serve the
Lord." (*See* Joshua 24:19.) He threw cold water over
their dedication. It is scriptural to challenge cheap dedication. Alexander Maclaren says, "The best way to
deepen and confirm good resolutions too swiftly formed

is to state very plainly the difficulty of keeping them." I have long since been disgusted with church members who promise God their devotion on the Sunday night of a revival only to forsake the revival by Friday night for a ball game!

On one occasion when many believed on our Lord, we read that He did not believe in them (same Greek word) because He knew what was in man (*see* John 2:23–25). Joshua reminded the people that God is holy and jealous. He will not look upon sin and He will not share the throne of our hearts with another. (*See* Joshua 24:20.) We are in a day when cheap grace is being preached with no repentance to begin with and no discipleship to follow. We need to be cured of shallow discipleship that has no root or depth as our Lord indicated in the parable of the sower, the seed, and the soil. Sometimes I think we church members have just about rededicated ourselves to death!

The revival under Joshua took place at Shechem. There was another revival at the same Shechem long before the days of Joshua. Jacob had wandered from Bethel to Shechem where his daughter Dinah got into trouble. His sons took vengeance on the Shechemites and Jacob was sorely distressed. Then God commanded him to return to Bethel and dwell there and make an altar unto the Lord. Jacob obeyed promptly, ordered his household to put away their strange gods, change their garments, and return to the place of blessing. (*See* Genesis, chapters 34 and 35.) Like Joshua, as for Jacob and his house, he would serve the Lord. He did not ask the family whether or not they wanted to go. He did not take a vote. He was not afraid of frustrating Junior. He simply announced that they were returning to Bethel. More fathers like that would answer a good many problems of broken homes and wayward youngsters.

The family obeyed, gave up their strange gods and earrings, which Jacob buried under an oak. If American homes and churches followed a similar procedure, we would fill all the national forests in the country with surrendered idols! Paul had a book burning at Ephesus and Savonarola witnessed a similar sight in Florence. We need also to change our garments. The garb many Christians wear needs to be brought back to New Testament standards of modesty. Also, our spiritual wardrobe is in bad shape; we wear the filthy rags of self-righteousness, the spotted garments of worldliness, and the gray vestments of compromise. The prodigal was received by the father just as he was, but he had to put on a new robe for fellowship; so must we.

Joshua was the head of the nation and the leader of God's covenanted people. Jacob was the head of a family. Together, they represent the nation, the church, and the home. Joshua did not lament what a failure Israel had been; he gloried in her past and called the people to return to the standard under which they had begun. Jacob did not apologize for his failure as a father; he ordered his family back to Bethel. It is fashionable nowadays to apologize for the failure of America, the church, and the home. Politicians, sociologists, educators, preachers, parents—everybody is doing it. I have never seen such a strange crowd as there is at the mourner's bench, weeping on one another's shoulders about how we have failed the young people; how we need to make amends for our stupid past; how we need to get with it and be relevant, involved, and meaningful—whatever that means. The magazines are full of it; television is full of it. It is the *in* thing to sob and sigh about it. The psychology of it is devastating, for the more we cringe and crawl and confess, the more impudent and arrogant this petted and spoiled generation becomes.

Frankly, I am not in the mood to join these Jeremiahs, berate the establishment, and apologize for America. I am proud of my country's illustrious past. It is still a land that people are trying to get into, not out of! I would like to load up all who like it better somewhere else and wave good-bye, as long as I could see them, while they sail for the land of their heart's desire. This is my country; may she always be right, but right or wrong, *my* country. No mother says, "My boy, as long as he's right, but when he is wrong, he is not my boy." God does not say, "This Christian is my child so long as he is right, but when he is wrong he is not my child." When my country is wrong it is my duty to call it back to God. Some things were wrong when I was a boy, but we did not try to burn down everthing we disliked because we were not prepared to put something better in its place. That is right for today as well.

I am not bemoaning the failure of the church. We are not called to preside at the funeral of Christianity. The church of Jesus Christ is not dead. The gates of hell shall not prevail against it. (*See* Matthew 16:18.) They say the church has failed in not updating her terminology, in her social program, in not getting through to youth. I will tell you where the church has failed; she has failed at the point of the inspiration of the Scriptures, the Lordship of Christ, the sovereignty of the Spirit, the separation from the world, and the discipleship. She has gone into religious socialism, building bigger and better hog pens in the far country instead of getting prodigals home to God. The world had more respect for the church when she was attending to her own business instead of making moral issues out of political projects.

I am thankful for my own denomination. I was pastor of the mother church of Southern Baptists and I know what they have stood for. I agree with one of their stal-

warts of the past who said, with reference to certain dis-
senters, "When they get right, they'll be with me for I'm
standing where they used to be." I have no intention of
leaving my denomination. If any people leave, let it be
the ones who do not believe what we used to believe.
The mutineers should not be allowed to take over the
ship. Some old-timers are accused of rocking the boat,
but it is better to rock the boat than to wreck it. Old-
fashioned Baptists should not leave the denomination;
we were here first. Nobody from headquarters has ever
told me what to preach. It would not make any difference if they did, but they have not.

If this sounds out-of-date, I can only say that after over
half a century of preaching, I still keep an itinerary of
preaching engagements booked two years ahead. If I am
a back number, I am not alone. More than seven thousand have not bowed to Baal! (*See* 1 Kings 19:18.)

What the church needs is a Joshua who will glory in
the blessings of the past and call on God's people to turn
from their idols to God. We are emphasizing everything
but revival, and that is a trick of the devil to keep us from
facing the real issue. If people in our great gatherings
spent their time emphasizing revival instead of
evangelism, seeking the joy of salvation restored and a
new spirit; then transgressors would be taught God's
ways, and sinners would be converted.

Back of the nation and the church lies the home. I offer
no apology for the old-fashioned home. We still have
some where father is the head and mother the heart instead of a two-headed monster. We still have some
homes where children are being brought up in the nurture and admonition of the Lord, but by and large,
America is a disaster area homewise. Nowhere has the
devil scored a greater success. The automobile took the
family out of the home, and television brought the world

into the home. Now age has surrendered to youth, and Jacob is no longer able to lead his family back to Bethel; they have become permanent residents of Shechem.

Back of the nation, the church, and the home stands the individual. We need Joshuas who have made the great decision, *as for me and my house, we will serve the Lord*, and who will call the nation and church away from idolatry to serve the Lord. We need Jacobs who have met God themselves and who can lead their families out of Shechem back to Bethel, the House of God—better still, to El Bethel, the God of the House of God.

5 Caleb's Decision

Give Me This Mountain!

Before 1492 one of the mottos of the Spanish Empire was *Ne Plus Ultra*, "No More Beyond." It was assumed that the limits of earth had already been determined; then Columbus discovered a new world and the old motto was outdated. The great explorer had discovered *more beyond*.

> Behind him lay the gray Azores,
>   Behind the Gates of Hercules;
> Before him not the ghost of shores,
>   Before him only shoreless seas.
> The Good Mate said, "Now must we pray,
>   For, lo, the very stars are gone;
> Brave Admiral, what shall I say?"
>   "Why say, Sail on, sail on and on!"
>   JOAQUIN MILLER, *Columbus*

And sail on they did through darkness and despair, through rebellion and near mutiny, until one black night they sighted land. Columbus believed there was *more beyond*.

The Israelites had been in the Promised Land for

years, but had not conquered it entirely. There yet remained very much land to be possessed. "And Joshua said unto the children of Israel, How long are ye slack to go to possess the land, which the Lord God of your fathers hath given you?" (Joshua 18:3.) They had started out well enough, but had grown tired of fighting and had decided to live in peaceful coexistence with their heathen neighbors.

"Now all these things happened unto them for ensamples: and they are written for our admonition, upon whom the ends of the world are come" (1 Corinthians 10:11). Canaan is a type of a victorious Christian experience through which we possess our possessions in Christ. The Epistle to the Hebrews is the Joshua of the New Testament. It tells us that there remains a rest to the people of God. (*See* Hebrews 4:9.) We were never meant to stand on Jordan's stormy banks casting a wishful eye to Canaan's fair and happy land, where our possessions lie. Some church members still live in Egypt. Some wander in the wilderness. Some live on samples of the fruit of the land. Others make a foray into Canaan now and then, but fear the giants of Anak and all the *-ites*, just as Israel feared Canaanites and Hittites and Amorites and Perizzites and Hivites and Jebusites. (*See* Numbers 13:1–3, 17–33.)

When the ten spies gave their adverse report, there was one man who was not suffering from a grasshopper complex. Caleb was the Columbus of the party. He believed there was more beyond. He said: "Let us go up at once, and possess it; for we are well able to overcome it." (*See* Numbers 13:30.) Too many Christians still live under the old Spanish motto *No More Beyond*, living on a fringe of Canaan instead of dwelling in Beulah Land. There remaineth a rest to the people of God, and we do not have to wait until death and go through a graveyard to reach it. We enter when we cease our own striving and straining and rest in a finished redemption as God rested from a finished creation. We rest in our Lord's finished work, while we labor harder than ever in His unfinished work; but we labor with His strength, not ours.

There have always been a few like Caleb who are not satisfied with less than all God has for His own. We read that he had another spirit. In our church life today, our greatest need is not another building, another program, another preacher, but *another spirit*. We were excited about going to the moon, perhaps to hide our embarrassment at not knowing how to live on earth. Yet the greatest of all unexplored worlds lies before us, the life that is hid with Christ in God. The average Christian has barely set foot on the fringe of that world. We are digging as never before into the treasures of the material universe; but in the spiritual world, we are still in kindergarten, although we should be in graduate school. We are producing astronauts while few have even sent up a trial balloon in the world of the spirit. There is a new frontier for you! The tragedy of our church life is that most of our members go to their graves having lived all their days on the edge of a spiritual continent. They might have explored that spiritual continent if they had followed the urging of Joshua to possess their possessions in Jesus Christ. We are short on Calebs with *another spirit!*

What kind of people does this call for? Caleb was eighty-five years old and he wholly followed the Lord his God. (*See* Joshua 14:8.) *He carried out a purpose*. He was not following with ifs, reservations, and provisos, with one hand behind his back and his fingers crossed; all of him was going in one direction.

Moreover, *he claimed a promise*. God had promised him a mountain and now he was laying claim to it. To him, a promise from God was not a motto to hang on a wall, but a check to cash, and now he was ready to cash it. He asked, *Give me this mountain!* He was not asking for a molehill, a pension, and soft retirement. This old soldier had no intention of just fading away! The mountain was Hebron, the stronghold of the Anakim, the giants who had scared the spies forty-five years before. They had seen a difficulty in every opportunity; Caleb saw an opportunity in every difficulty. Here is an old soldier at eighty-five, out to win the greatest prize of his life. He did not say, "I've had my day, I'll step aside and let youth take over while I reminisce about the good old days." He would make his batting average good to the end of the season and make a home run in the last inning!

Caleb not only carried out a purpose and claimed a promise, *he counted on a presence: If so be the Lord will be with me, then I shall be able to drive them out.* (*See* Joshua 14:12.) This *if* is not an *if* of doubt but of humility. He does not claim victory because he is brave or because he has wholly followed the Lord but *if God be with me*. We leave God out of our calculations these days. We say, "*If* we have enough education, ability, money, personality . . . ." It is not our efficiency but his sufficiency.

Then, *Caleb conquered a possession,* and it became Hebron, the city of refuge. There was a *quest;* he wholly followed God. There was a *request:* Give me this mountain! There was a *conquest:* he took the mountain. There was a *bequest:* Hebron became his inheritance.

Do not make up your mind that there is no more beyond. Be a Columbus on the ocean of God's grace. Better still, be a Caleb even in old age, not settling for a molehill but claiming a mountain. There are some pretty rugged mountains in our way these days. God give us men to match these mountains!

James tells us that we ask, and receive not, because we ask amiss, and he also says that we have not because we ask not. (*See* James 4:2, 3.) We ask for things we should not have, but we also could have many things we do not have because we do not ask for them. We settle for molehills when we could have mountains. Some years ago I felt led to make a three-fold prayer: like Hezekiah, I asked for *an extension of time* (*see* 2 Kings 20:1–6); like Jabez, I asked for *an enlargement of coast* (*see* 1 Chronicles 4:10); and, like Elisha, I asked for *an enduement of power* (*see* 2 Kings 2:9). That is a big order, but God likes to show us great and mighty things which we know not. There are so many frightened spies with scary reports of how many giants they have seen. God wants to honor the Calebs who select the headquarters of those giants for their target.

In old age we are tempted to go into the molehill business, but there is not much challenge in molehills. There is no better antidote for senility and no better medicine for hardening of the arteries than to ask God for a mountain!

Caleb made one all-inclusive decision: to wholly follow the Lord his God. That decision covered all other subsequent choices. When a man makes that high resolve, all else falls into place. Mountains that once stood in his way become his possession. But *wholly* means completely. There are no ifs and reservations and provisos. It is not half-hearted, part-time allegiance. We have filled our churches with laggards whose hearts are not in it. They feel like grasshoppers before the giants of Anak. We need some Calebs with another spirit; then we will be capturing mountains instead of stumbling over molehills.

Joshua and Caleb made a great team. We need both

today: Joshuas to call God's people to revival and Calebs to lead us in possessing our possessions—victorious living, spiritual conquest in the Promised Land. Today both the nation and the church have gone all out in their emphasis on youth and concessions to it. Much is being done for the aged but some wonder whether we should prolong life unduly when many become human vegetables. One thing is certain: many Christians become vegetables spiritually in old age. They ought to be Calebs, sturdy old soldiers who refuse to fade away, but insist on claiming the promises of God while others sit in retirement, content to reminisce. Caleb indeed remembered the past, but to him it was a bugle call in the present. He was not out to write memoirs, but to win mountains! Some old ministers think it is their duty to sit in a corner and let youth have its day. They offer no counsel, utter no warning, and remain silent on burning issues; they consider that a mark of Christian graciousness, but they miss the opportunity to render a great service. Indeed, they should not gripe about the times and lament the passing of the good old days, but they should demonstrate that Caleb has his place in the conquest of Canaan. There are Hebrons to be captured and giants of Anak to be slain, and few of these victories will ever be won by new recruits. Some victories are reserved for veterans who have wholly followed the Lord their God.

6 David's Decision

Doing Right the Wrong Way

David decided to bring the ark to Jerusalem. The Philistines had captured it during the last sad days of Eli. It caused them so much trouble that they put it on a cart and returned it, and for a while it stayed at the house of Abinadab. (*See* 1 Samuel 7:1.) David undertook to bring it to Jerusalem. His motive was good, but his method was wrong. He was right in his intentions but wrong in the implementation. God had ordered that the ark should be carried only on the shoulders of the Levites. David loaded it on a new cart to be drawn by oxen. He probably got the idea from the Philistines; so it was an expedient borrowed from the enemies of Israel. On the way the oxen stumbled, and when Uzzah put forth his hand to steady the ark, God struck him dead. (*See* 2 Samuel 6:2–8.)

This strange tragedy has some serious lessons for us today. Just as David borrowed his idea from the Philistines, the church today has borrowed from the world the vehicles of her ministry. We study the techniques of this age, the gadgetry of the business, social, and entertainment world, looking for new carts on which to carry the ark of our testimony. We hold a wet finger in the air to ascertain which way the popular wind is blowing; we set our sails to catch the latest breeze. Instead of asking,

"How does God do it?" we ask, "How does the world do it?" We are religious copycats; we mimic the manikins of this Punch-and-Judy show we call progress. We have called Hollywood to our aid as though the Gospel were a form of entertainment. Our worship is streamlined, our preaching slanted to tickle the ears of a generation that cannot endure sound doctrine.

When Uzzah tried to steady the ark, his intentions were good, but the whole procedure was wrong to start with. Today the ark reels and rocks, and Uzzah is worried. The brethren are disturbed about the unsteadiness of our doctrine, the wavering churches, the unstable swaying of modern Christianity. Sincere efforts are made to stabilize the situation, but they will end as Uzzah's did, in tragedy, for we have started out wrong. We must give up our new carts and get God's work on the shoulders of separated and dedicated people.

What was the sin of Uzzah? He had no regard for the sanctity of the ark. He was the son of Abinadab, and all his life he had seen the ark in his home. It was a familiar piece of furniture and had become to him just a box. Some of us grow so familiar with the Gospel, with the worship and ordinances of the church, that we lose our reverence. Alexander Maclaren says in his *Expositions of Holy Scriptures* that Uzzah had lost the sense of awe: "Nothing is more delicate than a sense of awe; trifle with it ever so little and it speedily disappears. There is far too little of it in our modern religion." Just watch any Sunday-morning congregation!

Uzzah had lost his regard for the sacredness of the ark as the symbol of God's presence among His people. In his *Commentary*, Matthew Henry puts it this way: "Perhaps he had affected to show before this great assembly how bold he could make with the ark, having been so long acquainted with it. Familiarity, even with that which is most awful, is apt to breed contempt."

It is a fearful thing to treat the ark as though it were a box! We can become so accustomed to being Christians and being preachers that we place unholy hands on sacred things. Our intentions may be good, but, as Matthew Henry says again: "It will not suffice to say of that which is ill done that it was well meant."

It is only because of the long-suffering of God that more corpses, like Uzzah's before the ark, do not lie around today. Even ministers of long experience may become so accustomed to their work that it becomes routine, and the holy awe departs. Growing up in Christian homes, we may easily mistake the *language* of Christianity for its *life* and become parrots of pious phrases. There is no greater hindrance to genuine spirituality than a superficial familiarity with Christianity from childhood. We get so accustomed to it that we play marbles with diamonds. We are hearing everywhere about relevance; we had better do something about reverence.

There is another angle to this episode. It may have been more sophisticated, up-to-date, and speedier—it actually took longer—to haul the ark on a cart, but it was not God's way. There was something personal about carrying the ark on the shoulders of the Levites; shifting to a cart lessened the sense of personal responsibility. Today the Lord's work has become impersonal. We let a machine do it. Putting our shoulders to the wheel is not the same thing as putting our shoulders under the ark. Too much of our giving is like feeding nickels into slots in a vending machine. It is a vain oblation when the Macedonians do not first give themselves. God wants self before service and substance. Fancy new Philistine carts may take a load from our shoulders, but we cannot transfer personal responsibility.

The problem was not that the oxen stumbled, the cart shook, and the ark lurched; there should have been no oxen and cart to begin with. No matter how many Uzzahs try to steady the ark, we are working on the wrong problem, and we are not going to help matters by making better carts and hiring trained Uzzahs. New ways to raise church money, to increase attendance, to interest the young people, new styles in church music—we never had so many new carts running all over the place, but never has the ark wobbled as it does today.

There was plenty of fanfare and music on this occasion, but it did not hide the fact that the whole arrangement was David's idea and not God's. We read that the thing was right in the eyes of all the people. (*See* 1 Chronicles 13:4.) But the voice of the people is not the voice of God. It is possible to put on an elaborate religious parade and have only a performance instead of an experience, a form of godliness without the power thereof.

David finally came to his senses. He was late getting around to it but better late than never. He began by recognizing that the ark should be carried only by Levites. He had broken that rule; that was at the bottom of all the trouble. The first thing we need to do in church these days is to discover that *God's work must be done by God's people in God's way.* A church cannot be run like a department store. Business and musical ability can be used only when dedicated and sanctified because they that are in the flesh cannot please God. (*See* Romans 8:8.) Only the Levites were qualified to carry the ark, and only separated and dedicated people can do the work of the church. Personality, education, ability, enthusiasm—all these glorify God only when empowered by the Holy Spirit.

So David had a convocation and gathered all Israel to

bring back the ark the right way the second time. We need to call such a meeting today, to summon God's people back to God's way of doing God's work. That is revival. David assembled the priests and Levites and charged them to sanctify themselves that they might bring up the ark of the Lord. (*See* 1 Chronicles 15:12.) We elect and appoint choir members, Sunday-school teachers, and deacons on the basis of ability, education, and position in the community, but we rarely ask, "Have they ever set themselves apart for the service of God?" I am amazed at the kinds of people I sometimes see working in the church—no wonder the ark wobbles!

Musicians were appointed for this occasion. If ever sanctified musicians were needed, it is today! The church has been invaded by gospel jazz, degenerating from hymns to hootenannies; church music has fallen upon evil days. Gospel singing is primarily a matter of heart rather than art, singing and making melody in our hearts to the Lord. A musical education can be dedicated to God; it stands to reason that a trained voice can sing better than an untrained voice, but in the last analysis, when it comes to glorifying God, what makes the difference is whether the singer, trained or untrained, is a separated, dedicated, Spirit-filled Christian. We are in a world where the standards of this age do not apply, no matter how gifted, popular, or successful one may be in the eyes of men.

When David finally brought the ark back to Jerusalem, it was a time of great rejoicing. It is always such a time when God's work is done by God's people God's way. That is revival. But Michal, David's wife, did not rejoice. She was Saul's daughter and had bad blood in her veins. She despised the king and met him with satire and scorn. (*See* 2 Samuel 6:16.) As a result, she suffered the shame of barrenness for the rest of her life. When revival comes, there will always be Michals who find fault. When our Lord cleansed the temple, there was great rejoicing, but the Pharisees voiced bitter protest. (*See* Mark 11:15–18.) Such people are already smitten with spiritual barrenness and bear no fruit to the glory of God.

The biggest business before the church today is to get the work of God off the new carts, the Philistine-like expedients of our own devising, and back on the shoulders of separated men and women. Too many Philistines run the churches today. The world has gotten into Sunday-school classes, choirs, offices, and pulpits. The ark is shaking and Uzzahs are trying to steady it. The whole procedure is wrong and we need to call a convocation and start over. We do not need something new; we need something so old that it will seem new!

God's work must be done by God's people in God's way. They that are in the flesh cannot please God, and no flesh can glory in His presence. The church has become an Old Adam Improvement Society. Having begun in the Spirit, we would perfect ourselves in the flesh. Old Adam is walking down church aisles rededicating himself, but God does not accept the old nature and cannot use old Adam, no matter how much he rededicates himself. God uses only men and women who have died and have risen with Christ to walk in newness of life. That which is born of the flesh is flesh and that which is born of the Spirit is spirit and only the twice-born can serve God in spirit and in truth. We have rededicated ourselves to death and to no purpose, because the wrong people are doing the rededicating.

God ordered that the anointing oil should not be poured on man's flesh, that none should be compounded like it, and that it should not be put on strangers (*see* Exodus 30:30–33). We cannot anoint old Adam for God's service. Imitation worship, praise, and joy are anathema to Him, for the unction of the Spirit cannot be prepared in the apothecaries of the natural man. To make old Adam into a deacon or teacher or minister is to anoint a stranger.

Ezekiel's valley of dry bones is with us today. (*See* Ezekiel 37:1–10.) We hold dry-bones conventions where church experts, with briefcases full of graphs and charts, lecture on how to rearrange dry-bones church members into new designs, but there is still no flesh on them and no breath in them. We have dry-bones specialists for each bone: jaw-bone experts, collar-bone, knee-bone, ankle-bone, any-bone experts with beautiful new arrangements for bones of all ages; but still there is no flesh on them and no breath in them. We need to prophesy to the bones and to the wind until there is a mighty shaking and these dry bones live.

Church members need to ask themselves three searching questions. *Am I one of God's people?* Much of our church work is being done by people who have never been born again. If they are what they have always been, they are not Christians. Christians are a purchased people, not their own, but bought with a price, a different people because they belong to a new race. *Am I doing God's work?* I do not mean church work alone, but living for Christ every day everywhere. Much of our church work may not be God's work. He may never have started it and may have nothing to do with it. Pastors are often kept busy doing things God never called them to do. *Am I doing God's work God's way?* Why do we do what we do? Is God working in us or is it unsanctified flesh, glorying in His presence, trying to please Him?

When God's people do God's work God's way, that will be revival, and David will get the ark back to Jerusalem.

7 Rehoboam's Decision

Shields of Brass

There is no sadder record in all the Bible than the account of the rise and fall of Solomon. No man ever got off to a more auspicious start, and no man ever came to a more disappointing finish. The headings of the chapters concerning Solomon's career run an ascending scale: Solomon's accession; Solomon's prayer for wisdom; Solomon builds the temple; Solomon's great wisdom; Solomon's wealth and splendor—and then, suddenly, Solomon's heart turned away from Jehovah. But Solomon's downfall was no instant collapse; men do not fold up all at once. The beginnings of Solomon's ruin date back to his affinity with Pharaoh and his love of strange women. No man ever lived in greater luxury, but mortal man is not built to withstand prosperity. Even a good man, while he may be secure in danger, is endangered by security. No nation can endure opulence for long.

> Ill fares the land, to hastening ills a prey,
> Where wealth accumulates, and men decay.
> **OLIVER GOLDSMITH**

Today America is spiritually sick, starving in the midst of abundance, a nation of paupers in a land of plenty.

53

Even the church cannot endure affluence; she becomes
rich and increased with goods and, needing nothing,
knows not that she is wretched and miserable and poor
and blind and naked. Times like the days of Solomon do
not breed great leaders. Adversity may produce a Moses,
a Joshua, a David, but out of the days of Solomon came
Rehoboam. He is the only son of Solomon mentioned in
the Scriptures. He had grown up in all the luxury and
corruption of Solomon's decline. He must have been a
spoiled brat. He was totally unfit to shoulder the great
responsibilities put on him at the death of his father.

The kingdom was threatened with division; rebellion
was in the air. The people of the Ten Tribes were rising
in protest. Rehoboam was faced with a momentous decision. He consulted the older men, who advised a gentle
policy toward the opposition; then he conferred with the
younger men, who recommended harsh and violent
measures. He decided in favor of the younger set, and
the kingdom split in two leaving Rehoboam with only
the tribes of Judah and Benjamin.

We are living in a day when protest and dissension
imperil the nation. The counsel of age is being rejected
in favor of the demands of youth. Of course, Rehoboam
was in his forties and so were most of his younger advis-
ers, but the general principle holds. He forsook the sober
voice of experience and listened to the folly of immaturity.

Today we adults are outnumbered by the new generation. Parents are afraid of their children; teachers are
afraid of their students; and politicians tremble before
these soon-to-be voters. It is true that only a small per-
centage of youth are radicals, but it was only small
minorities that sparked the French and Bolshevik Rev-
olutions.

The older generation with its permissiveness; the lack

of discipline in home, school, and church; the ridiculous new ideas in child training: all these have sown the wind, and now we reap the whirlwind. The old generation has adjusted to the new, renounced its own standards, and changed its convictions. Even Christian parents have broken down, trying to accommodate to way-out youth, and all are going down together. Instead of age molding youth, it is now the other way around. There is as much authority in the home as ever, but the children wield it.

Some things require time; there are some things that youth does not know simply because it has not been here long enough. It makes a lot of difference whether we are growing oaks or mushrooms. It takes more than long hair, sideburns, a medallion, and a guitar to qualify for world leadership. The newest approach—cutting off the hair and lobbying in Washington—may appear better, but if Rehoboam listens to it, he will see the kingdom divided. I remember a motto in an old country doctor's office: It's what you learn after you know it all that counts!

Recently I watched a group of preteenagers discussing the problems of the day on a television panel. Not content with symposiums of high schoolers on national issues, we are almost ready to rob the cradle. What a sight to behold—children discussing ecology and the generation gap, when they should have been playing hopscotch in the backyard! Let the experts mull over these weighty matters. They do not know much more than the kids, but at least, they have had their childhood. Why drag these babes away from their toys into such ordeals before their time? It is rough enough to be adults, when we have to be; it is a crime to steal a youngster's childhood. These are the same kids whose mothers rush them off to dates and dances and try to make precocious freaks out of nor-

mal happy children. Give them the few precious years
when life is less fact than fancy. All too soon they must
enter the old salt mines and start the rat race.

This current abnormal catering to youth can only result in turning out a flock of young Absaloms like the
wild young son of David, who thought all the ills of
society could be cured by revolt. It will be a fine day
when the youths who condemn hypocrisy and dishon-
esty in adults give us a demonstration of their own at-
titudes toward God, Christ, and the church, a demonstration of the virtues they do not see in us.

Today youth dominates the home and makes the major
decisions. Youth dominates many churches; the youth
program becomes the tail that wags the dog. At the present rate, deacons may eventually be chosen from the
junior department! Teenage voters will soon make themselves felt in the nation. We are developing a teenage
culture and society with immature standards and goals.
Everything is geared to the whims of youth. In the
churches, pastors, assistants, teachers, and parents shake
their heads and say, "We don't know where all this is
going and we can't make up our minds about the new
religious music." Well, we ought to know what we think
and what to say. It is our duty to understand, direct, and
counsel. We never so much as today needed the gift to
discern the spirits, whether they be of God. Uncertainty
in adults encourages rebellion in youth. If we are afraid
to speak for fear we might be wrong, it is quickly sensed,
and the reaction is certain.

The way we frantically plunge in all directions trying
every fad to popularize the Gospel would be comical if it
were not so tragic. Ichabod Memorial Church packs
them in with a folk musical; then *Ephesus* (*see* Revela
tion 1:11) puts on a television celebrity. Everybody
starts looking for a bigger star for their show. *Pergamos*

puts on a freak musician who can play a fiddle, beat trap drums with his feet, and play a harmonica all at the same time. *Sardis* puts on an old-fashioned Aunt Dinah's quilting party where everyone goes to see Nellie home. *Laodicea*, not to be outdone, features a talking horse that stomps with its foot ten times when asked how many Commandments there are, twelve times when asked how many apostles. (Somebody says facetiously he was asked, "How many hypocrites are there in this church?" and went into a dance on all fours!)

One is reminded of the skinny razorback hogs in Arkansas. Their sad plight was explained by their owner, who said, "I used to knock on the fence when I fed them corn, and they came running. But there are a lot of woodpeckers around now, and every time one drums on a limb, the hogs take off in that direction, expecting more corn. They have just about killed themselves running all over the lot." Today every church entertainer gets a crowd of razorbacks who are exhausting themselves trying to make all the church vaudeville shows and religious night clubs.

What would happen if some desperate pastor and a few faithful members decided to try God and the Gospel, wait on God in penitent, persevering prayer, until the heavens were opened and the power came down? If heaven has gone out of business and the Book is no longer true, we might as well lock up the churches. If God ever rends the heavens and returns in revivalist blessing, we are going to be red in the face with embarrassment because we ever sank so low as to call in the world, the flesh, and the devil to popularize the Gospel.

We need age to keep us from going too fast and youth to keep us from going too slow. It has been said that youth has fire without light and age has light without fire. Someone said, "If only youth knew how to live and old age could!" If youth knows how to run the universities, why are they going to school? When immaturity and inexperience take over the university, the church, or the country, there can be only disaster. This is an impatient, nervous, frantic generation that cannot wait. We would tear open the cocoon before the butterfly is ready. More things than coffee need to percolate awhile. Our Lord waited for thirty years before He began His ministry. Ephraim was like a cake not turned. (*See* Hosea 7:8.) We have too many half-baked Ephraims today in positions of responsibility, nor do they cover up being half-baked by acting hard-boiled!

Youthful exuberance must be tempered with the wisdom of age. Youth revivals in our churches can be a great blessing, but they can also get out of hand. The new music now heard in our churches is a threatening menace and must be controlled lest hymns give way to hootenannies. Back of much of the modern, youthful unrest is Communism, paganism, and even demonism. Dark forces from the unseen world of evil are manipulating projects that bear the sanction of organized religion. It is the day of perplexity predicted by our Lord, and the wisest minds—to say nothing of inexperienced youth—need a double portion of God's Spirit to find the way.

Not all young people are to be found in the radical and rebellious ranks today. There are thousands who are living dedicated Christian lives. They do not get on television and make headlines in these perverted times. I have better listening and response among our youth today, after over half a century of preaching, than I ever had before. Some of the things I read and hear sound as though young people had just been invented! They can be our greatest asset or our greatest liability. We must be sensible and recognize that they are not ready for some responsibilities simply because some things require

time, seasoning, and maturity; young people have not
lived long enough to acquire these. Age has been both
young and old in its time; youth has only been young.
Any Rehoboam who tries to run the kingdom on the
counsel of youth alone will divide his domain and invite
disaster.

Things went from bad to worse under Rehoboam:
Judah did evil in the sight of the Lord; they provoked
Him to jealousy; they built high places and images and
groves; there were sodomites in the land; and Judah did
according to all the abominations of the heathen nations
(*see* 1 Kings 14:21–27). On the heels of this apostasy,
Shishak, king of Egypt, attacked Jerusalem and took
away the treasures of God's house including the shields
of gold that Solomon had made. Solomon was definitely
on the gold standard. None of the vessels of the house of
the forest of Lebanon were of silver; it was nothing ac-
counted of in the days of Solomon (*see* 1 Kings 10:21).
We read that when Shishak stole the shields of gold,
Rehoboam made shields of brass in their stead. Not even
silver but brass! What a comedown! How embarrassed
the people of Jerusalem must have been when they
showed the temple to their visiting friends! "We have
seen better times. Once golden shields hung here, but
now we have only brass."

The church has been robbed of her golden shields.
Instead of admitting it and seeking a return to gold or
nothing, we are polishing brass these days. Brass will
shine, but it is not gold. Like Rehoboam we would substitute the good for the best. The world knows we have
been robbed. We deceive nobody but ourselves. So
much of our worship is brass. We have brass revivals.
How much of our religious activity is brass, a pitiful substitute for the real thing! We are not even willing to
admit that it is brass. We stoutly and stubbornly insist on

a cheaper brand of Christianity rather than pay the price and recover our shields of gold.

You will observe that although Rehoboam sought the advice of both age and youth, nowhere do we read that he sought the help of God. Other kings, like Asa, Jehoshaphat, and Hezekiah turned to the Lord in times of crisis, but not Rehoboam. We perfunctorily ask God's help sometimes in formal prayers, but there is no desperate turning to heaven for help as Jehoshaphat did when he said, "We know not what to do but our eyes are upon Thee." (*See* 2 Chronicles 20:12.) When we start out relying on the arm of flesh, we are not likely to call upon God in dead earnest.

Both in the nation and in the church we are making Rehoboam's decision and repeating his mistake. The consequences will be brass instead of gold. In America the sturdy qualities that made us great, the love of our flag and country, have given way to a new cheap internationalism leavened with Communism. Patriotism is despised and the flag is spat upon. In the church we have a Christless churchianity and a churchless Christianity, a form of godliness without power, form without force, ritual without righteousness. Shishak has robbed the temple. If we ever are to recover our golden shields, we must revoke our foolish decisions, regain our sanity, and seek counsel first, from neither age nor youth, but from our God.

8 Elijah's Decision

Showdown on Carmel

By *Elijah's Decision* I mean the choice he called upon Israel to make: "How long halt ye between two opinions? if the Lord be God, follow him: but if Baal, then follow him." (*See* 1 Kings 18:21.)

Elijah, that solitary prophet of God, broke out of the woods to announce three years of dry weather. When he appeared again, famine was raging in Samaria. It had rained on neither the just nor the unjust. In the eighteenth chapter of First Kings, rain is promised in verse 1 and provided in verse 45, but between those verses, preparation was made for showers of blessing. Rain is a symbol of the favor of God in revival. Shut up heaven that there be no rain (*see* Deuteronomy 11:17) is a figure of spiritual drought. We live in such a drought today. There is a famine of the hearing of the words of the Lord, partly because it cannot be heard and partly because so many will not hear it. The drama on Mount Carmel sets before us a pattern for spiritual revival. In order to understand that pattern, we must study the background and the characters that move upon this scene.

First, there was that rugged man of God, Elijah. Spiritual awakenings usually are spearheaded by a prophet. Elijah was no superman; he was subject to the same passions as we are, but he prayed, and prayed earnestly, and in that, he outstrips us. He could pray down fire or water. We need both today, the fire of the Spirit and showers of revival. He got ready for his mission by the brook Cherith (*see* 1 Kings 17:3) as did Paul in Arabia (*see* Galatians 1:17). Every man of God needs a session by the brook before going into battle.

Then there were Ahab, the weakling, and the notorious Jezebel. (*See* 1 Kings 16:29–33; 17:1–6; 18:4, 13.) They set up the worship of Baal in Israel, and through Athaliah, they did the same in Judah. Jezebel was one of the most wicked women on record. She persecuted the prophets of the Lord and frightened even the sturdy Elijah; so that he took off for the wilderness. In Revelation 2:18–23, we read of another Jezebel, in the church at Thyatira. The church is still plagued with her kind. She would mix the church with the world, join the altar of Jehovah with the altar of Baal, the mystery of godliness with the mystery of lawlessness. She hates prophets, and when Elijah calls for a showdown on Carmel, she wants to murder him on the spot. She teaches and seduces Christians to commit spiritual adultery, forgetting that they are married to Christ, espoused to one spiritual husband. Our Lord condemned the church for suffering—tolerating—Jezebel. We do the same today, and God judges us as much by what we allow as by what we practice. We need a prophet to call the church to decision between Jehovah and Baal, between Christ and Belial.

On the way to meet Ahab, Elijah found Obadiah, who was a good man but lined up with Ahab looking for grass, when he should have been with Elijah praying for rain. It is true that Obadiah hid one hundred prophets in a cave, but prophets that must be hidden in a cave probably would not be worth much in broad daylight! Obadiah was a religious politician trying to work both sides of the street. If Israel had turned to God, it would not have been necessary to send out grass-hunting expeditions. It is not necessary to look for grass when God sends rain, but there will be no showers, until first there is a show-down. There is spiritual famine today and some well-meaning church leaders are trying to alleviate the drought by social reforms and government projects under church auspices. We are oversupplied with Obadiahs, but are woefully short on prophets who can stand on Carmel and call God's people to repentance. A little grass may be discovered now and then by Obadiah's foragers, but it is not God's way to relieve drought and famine. We have no business entangling ourselves with the affairs of this life and becoming infected with the futile enthusiasms of this age. Glorified socialism under the banner of the church is not the answer to our ills today. It is more popular to stand in with the powers that be and team up with Ahab instead of taking one's place with lonely Elijah. Today church convocations spend much of their time trying to work out a grass-hunting program when every one of them ought to turn into a showdown on Carmel, praying down fire and water from heaven. God has plainly told us that if He withholds rain, He will send showers of blessing when His people humble themselves, pray, seek His face, and turn from their wicked ways.

The difference between Obadiah and Elijah was this Obadiah tried to remedy the situation from within the establishment; Elijah sought to change it from without. Obadiah lacked conviction and courage, for otherwise he would never have had a job in Ahab's administration. He reminds us of Lot in Sodom. Both men were vexed and shocked by what they saw—Obadiah in Samaria and Lot in Sodom—but neither of them changed the situation.

Dr. F. B. Meyer said: "There is not a single hero or saint whose name sparkles on the inspired page, who moved his times from within: all, without exception, have raised the cry, 'Let us go forth without the camp.' " They tell us today, "Stay in the world, join its clubs, attend its festivities, copy its styles and fashions." That is like a good woman marrying a bad man in order to reform him. The man who joins the world to level it up will find himself leveled down. The church that marries the world becomes worldy instead of making the world become Christian. The times do not need an Obadiah, but an Elijah, to confront Ahab and call for a showdown on Carmel. Archimedes said he could move the earth if he had somewhere to stand. Men who have moved the world have not done it from within: their lever was rested on a fulcrum without.

"And it came to pass, when Ahab saw Elijah, that Ahab said unto him, Art thou he that troubleth Israel? And he answered, I have not troubled Israel; but thou, and thy father's house, in that ye have forsaken the commandments of the Lord and thou hast followed Baalim" (1 Kings 18:17, 18). That put the shoe on the right foot; yet Elijah *was* a troubler of Israel, one in that noble succession of disturbers of the peace who, through the ages, have kept nations off the rocks and God's people from slumbering their time away. They have aroused sanctuary sleepers, given wicked rulers insomnia, and brought discomfort to the palaces of the mighty. How we need troublers of Israel today! William Barclay says: "The settled ministry began to resent the intrusion of these wandering prophets who often disturbed their congregations." Amos was not chummy with Jeroboam II. John the Baptist was not a guest in Herod's palace. Paul was a prisoner in Caesar's jail, but not Caesar's prisoner!

Ahab was the troublemaker, but Elijah was the troubleshooter. Big business employs such men to look out for bugs and breakdowns. God has such men in the church. They have an instinct for locating trouble and a genius for exposing it. Naturally, they are not popular. It is much more pleasant to be a Gamaliel (*see* Acts 5:34–36) keeping everything quiet in Jerusalem than to be a Paul exceedingly troubling Philippi (*see* 1 Thessalonians 2:2). Such men play havoc with the serenity school and irritate the tranquilizers. Just when false prophets of peaceful coexistence have lulled everybody to rest, at ease in Zion, the prophet blasts the neighborhood with a siren that cries aloud and spares not.

When Elijah called for a decision, "How long halt ye between two opinions?" the people answered him not a word. Whether from fear of Ahab and Jezebel, because they would not renounce their idols, or they were waiting to see how this showdown on Carmel turned out, they were a fifth-amendment, noncommittal crowd who would not take a stand. It reminds us of the crowd at our Lord's Crucifixion. We read in Matthew 27:36, "And sitting down they watched him there." Imagine sitting as if at a circus or play, watching the Son of God die for the sins of the world! During the French Revolution some women took their knitting to the guillotines and sat watching the beheadings, but that is nothing compared to the spectators at the cross. *Were you there when they crucified my Lord?* Yes, we were all there; we had a hand in it; we are not onlookers. Too often church congregations sit on Sunday morning as if to watch a performance, and when the preacher calls for decision, they answer not a word. Spectatoritis, whether at Carmel or Calvary or anywhere else, is despicable in the sight of God.

We are beset by neutralism, drugged by moral inertia,

immobilized by spiritual paralysis. It is a strange age
trying to live in a third dimension as though there were a
no-man's-land between right and wrong, heaven and
hell. There will never be revival as long as the church
avoids a showdown, merges black and white into grey,
sets up the altar of Baal beside the altar of Jehovah, pro-
fesses faith in Jesus, and tolerates Jezebel.

Elijah proposed the test of fire. "The God that
answereth by fire, let Him be God." (*See* 1 Kings 18:24.)
Not figures and finances or fame or feelings, but *fire*, not
a painted Pentecost, not strange fire, or stage fire, but
Spirit fire. There is plenty of fire loose in the world, and
much of it is not divine but demonic. There are false fires
in the church and flames we have kindled in the flesh
(*see* Isaiah 50:11). Some find it difficult to determine
which fire is from heaven and which is from hell. Satan
imitates the work of God, but the counterfeit must not
frighten us away from the true. The supreme test is the
fire test. The God who answers by fire, let Him be God!

Elijah repaired the altar of God that was broken down.
There never was a revival that did not begin the rebuilding of broken altars of consecration, of family altars, of
altars of praise and testimony. Stained glass windows,
robed choirs, eloquence in the pulpit, and elegance in
the pew have never deceived God. He demands truth in
the inward parts, and heaven will keep silent until we
approach Him with rebuilt altars.

There must be sacrifice upon those altars—not a sacrifice for sin, for that has been offered once for all. There
must be the *sacrifice of penitence:* "The sacrifices of
God are a broken spirit: a broken and a contrite heart, O
God, thou wilt not despise" (Psalms 51:17). How little of
that do we see in our dry-eyed churches! There must be
the *sacrifice of person:* Present your bodies a living sacrifice (*see* Romans 12:1). The Macedonians first gave

themselves unto the Lord. A little boy had no money to give to church, but he wrote upon a slip of paper, "I give myself" and put that on the plate. And that was the biggest gift that morning!

> Lord Jesus, look down from Thy throne in the skies
> And help me to make a complete sacrifice;
> I *give up myself* and whatever I know;
> Now wash me and I shall be whiter than snow.

There must be the *sacrifice of praise*: "By him therefore let us offer the sacrifice of praise to God continually, that is, the fruit of our lips giving thanks to his name" (Hebrews 13:15). We try to work up that sacrifice by artificial means; song leaders sweat and plead trying to bring out a song that is not there. You cannot change the order of *penitence, person, praise*. When God's people repent and give themselves to God they will have a song. It will be spontaneous, for what is down in the well will come up in the bucket.

Elijah poured twelve barrels of water over the altar and the offering. (*See* 1 Kings 18:32–34.) I have never heard anybody even mention that detail. He did not warm up the altar to make it easier for God to consume the offering. We try to help God out by fleshly devices. Elijah made it as difficult as possible; so that God would get all the glory. He wanted nobody to suspect that there was a trick about it, fire hidden somewhere. He set the stage so that God would be the only performer. Today we decorate the altar instead of drenching it, but it is only the drenched altar that God sets on fire. We need twelve barrels of water poured over most of our religious activity; then if the fire falls, it will have to be supernatural! Flesh glories in His presence and we never seem to learn that they that are in the flesh cannot please God (*see* Romans 8:8). If Elijah had started a little blaze of his own, God would not have touched that sacrifice. When he did what he could do and should have done and called on God in holy desperation; then the fire fell.

When everything was finally in order, Elijah prayed: ". . . Lord God of Abraham, Isaac, and of Israel, let it be known this day that thou art God in Israel, and that I am thy servant, and that I have done all these things at thy word. Hear me, O Lord, hear me, that this people may know that thou art the Lord God, and that thou hast turned their heart back again." (1 Kings 18:36, 37.) Elijah was not on Carmel to demonstrate what he could do, but what *God* could do. We read in the next verse the fire of the Lord fell. Soon Elijah said, "There is a sound of abundance of rain." The fire and the flood! This is the divine order of revival: a prophet calling God's people back to God; a showdown with the forces of evil; the rebuilding of broken altars; the sacrifices on the altar; supplication in desperate prayer; then the fire of God's power and the flood of God's blessing!

If we ever needed that fire and that flood, now is the time. But we are not ready for a showdown on Carmel. There are too many Obadiahs. We are out for summit conferences, not confrontations; grass-hunting expeditions are the order of the day. Our great church gatherings come and go. Some good things are said, resolutions are passed, but we are operating on a business-as-usual basis in a world on fire. Some say: "We don't have time to put on a revival in our conventions." *We don't have time for anything else!* It is too late! Some say, "We are here to attend to business." *What greater business is there than to rebuild broken altars and offer the sacrifices of penitence, person, and praise?* When we do that and call on God in holy desperation, if we ever do, then the fire will fall, and there will be the sound of abundance of rain.

We are beset today with false gospels of liberalism, of secularism, of socialism under church auspices. Great denominations are deteriorating and degenerating. Some have adopted standards of morality that ought to make even infidels blush. The inspiration of God's Word is denied. The church has married the world. Social reform will not get us out of the woods. A return to theological orthodoxy is not enough; the Pharisees were orthodox and separated from the world, but they gave our Lord more trouble than all the publicans and sinners. Evangelism is not enough; the first items on God's program for the church today are repentance, confession of sin, cleansing, separation from the world, submission to Christ's Lordship, and the filling of the Spirit, but we politely dodge all that in our convocations. Elijah did not call a conference of Ahab, Jezebel, the priests of Baal, and Obadiah; he stood alone; and yet he was not alone, for seven thousand had not bowed to Baal. Today there is still a remnant and a cloud the size of a man's hand. Even Elijah ran away from the revival that started at Carmel; so it died aborning. God grant us a visitation that can withstand the threats of Jezebel!

9　Jehoshaphat's Decision

Teaming Up With the Ungodly

Jehoshaphat, King of Judah, was a good man, but easily influenced. Twice in his career he aligned himself with unholy men saying both times, "I am as thou art, my people as thy people, my horses as thy horses." (*See* 1 Kings 22:4; 2 Kings 3:7.) The objectives in both cases were worthy, but Ahab and Jehoram, with whom he teamed up, were unworthy. On both occasions, Jehoshaphat asked, "Is there not here a prophet of the Lord that we might enquire of him?" (*See* 1 Kings 22:7; 2 Kings 3:11.) He was aware of the need for divine guidance but he had entangled himself in an unwise confederacy. His two decisions to team up with evil men illustrate the dangers that accompany that fallacious notion that *the end justifies the means.*

We have never had so many Jehoshaphats in the leadership of the church as now. Good men they may be, and with the best of intentions, but they make alliances with the world to achieve their purposes. If the goal is desirable, it is assumed that the means are sanctified thereby. All sorts of tricks, devices, and gadgets, for instance, are brought in from the social, business, and entertainment world to attract people to hear the Gospel. If somebody is converted, that is supposed to put a halo around the means employed. Now God honors His Word, but we are not to infer that He always approves of the setup for the preaching of it. When Jehoshaphat joins Ahab in expeditions to Ramoth-gilead, it makes a lone dissenter of Micaiah, conspicuous as an odd number, particularly when four hundred false prophets say, Go up and prosper. (*See* 1 Kings 22:8–37.)

The end does not justify the means because the *means may determine the end.* There may be some temporary benefits in such mixed ventures, but in the long run, the result is weakening to the church. The whole enterprise is colored by the leavening of evil influences. The entire project is spoiled when questionable means are used to achieve its purpose. There is but one answer to the old question: Let us do evil that good may come of it? (*see* Romans 3:8). God's work must be done by God's people God's way, and God never teams up with the devil.

Jehoshaphat's policy shows up today in new social action programs of the church. A television magazine in an article titled "God and Man on TV" says, "Social concerns overwhelm spiritual ones in networks' religious programs." One church official laments rightly, "We've been trading in our Christianity for mere humanism." We have joined forces with this age; we are as they are, our people as their people, our horses as their horses—to use the language of Jehoshaphat. We may get uneasy sometimes, as he did, and ask whether there is a prophet of the Lord on hand of whom we may enquire. Micaiahs are hard to find these days when prophets find it more popular to stand in with Ahab and bid him go up against Ramoth-gilead and prosper. And who dares say a word against modern Jehoshaphats?

Christianity is now engulfed in a tidal wave of social reform. A deluge of books, articles, and sermons declares that the church is finally getting around to her main business and waking up to her true mission. She has majored too long on the vertical man-to-God relationship, we are told, and is now giving thought to the long-neglected horizontal man-to-man relationship. It is now the "in" thing to be socially involved with race, poverty, and housing. Conventions, congresses, and conclaves are sounding boards for the new socialism under religious auspices. Good men and great denominations are swept off their feet by the avalanche and stampeded by the surge.

One would gather from all this furor that heretofore Christianity has done next to nothing to alleviate suffering, help the needy, and improve the community. Any reader of history well knows that the church has done more for the betterment of mankind than all other institutions put together. One has only to read such books as *This Freedom, Whence?* by J. Wesley Brendy to know that the Wesleyan Revival started a social revolution that made an impact on all areas of society. The churches' ministry is teaching, healing, doing good, caring for the widows and orphans, campaigning for better living standards, making war on social unrighteousness—all this is common knowledge and has been through the centuries. Of course we should do good to all men: heal the sick, make conditions as good as we can, fight injustice, oppression, and lawlessness, and work for cleaner politics, honest business, and better homes. Faith without works is dead. A true Christian is a better parent, neighbor, citizen, or businessman; this is the outward expression of an inner experience, the outflow and overflow of a Spirit-filled life. My father never heard of sociology, but he was for better education, better roads, better politics. He was a Christian vertically and horizontally.

If the new social emphasis were a revival of this, we

would heartily endorse it, for Christianity has been weak in the outliving of the inliving Christ. We can understand how young idealists feel impatience and disgust with the dull, stodgy indifference of Sunday-morning congregations to the need of this world. Most of our church members could care less. They are both in and of the world; they do not gather with the Lord, instead they scatter, driving people away by their godless living. I can understand how any new Christian could condemn a smug, snug Christianity, insulated and isolated in its cathedrals from a suffering and lost humanity. Certainly the salt of the earth must be rubbed into the decaying carcass of society, but most church members would not touch it with a forty-foot pole. Forgetting that they *are* the disinfectant they are too refined and dainty to minister to this sinful race until it has been disinfected. Although I do not agree with them, I can see how reformers might feel that the religious establishment has had its day and that we need only dedicated bands who will infiltrate the social structure and the world culture. In their reaction to a Christless churchianity, they propose a churchless Christianity. They are mistaken and muddled, and their solution will not work, but I can see how they came to revolt against the religious status quo.

The new social movement, however, is a dangerous project with socialistic undertones and overtones. More political than spiritual, it is an effort to superimpose the kingdom of heaven on an unregenerate society by education, legislation, and reformation. It is a phase of the coming world-church, the Babylon of Revelation. Well does Dr. Thomas F. Torrance say in *The Apocalypse Today:* "When the church begins to stress community and social cohesion, it is a sign that she is losing her grip on the living God and is binding herself together in a collective magnitude in order to make up for internal bankruptcy."

It is also a matter of eschatology. If the world is to grow worse, if anarchy, apostasy, and apathy are to increase until Christ returns suddenly to set up His kingdom, that is one thing. But if Christianity is to infiltrate the world until it controls the structure of the age, that is something else. The new social upsurge proceeds on the second premise. Certainly Christians are to improve conditions, creating as much peace and good will as possible, but it must be within the framework and context of God's program in history. The church is not an accompanist but a soloist. It has its own role in the world but not as a waterboy to world revolution, to pronounce the blessing over government-sponsored and sociologically oriented projects for creating a false millennium.

The Word of God set the correct order long ago with the two commandments thou shalt love the Lord thy God and thy neighbor as thyself. We are in great danger of teaming up with movements and organizations and welfare projects that make much of loving one's neighbor, but know nothing of love for God as made known by Jesus Christ and the love of God shed abroad by the Holy Spirit. Our Lord set the record straight when He said: "But seek ye first the kingdom of God, and his righteousness; and all these things shall be added unto you" (Matthew 6:33). *All these things* meant food and clothing, those necessities so fussed about today.

The early church faced the same issue when the apostles refused to be diverted from preaching the Word to serving tables in order to meet the material needs of the fellowship. (*See* Acts 6:2.) If this priority was to hold within the church, certainly it would hold with regard to ministering to the world outside. The needs of society in general are the concern of the government, and Christians can work through agencies ordained for that purpose. When the church undertakes serving all kinds of tables for social relief and welfare, she forgets her main business and degenerates into an operator of soup kitchens and welfare projects. Ministering to the material needs of men is the outflow and overflow of the Spirit of God in the lives of Christians, but when it becomes the main activity of the church, she soon becomes another humanitarian do-good enterprise, no different from secular organizations organized for that sole purpose.

Dr. Nelson Bell writes: "The 'wave of the future,' so joyfully acclaimed by some churchmen, may prove to be a wave not of progress but of disaster. I am convinced that there are many good men caught up in the excitement of new-wave activity who have little idea of what it is they are supporting and where it is leading the church. I am equally convinced that there is a hard core of brilliant designers and coordinators who know exactly what they are doing and where they plan to take the church."

The good doctor is right. I am persuaded that many earnest and well-meaning Christians are being deceived on this point by him who would lead astray the very elect. They are being taken for a ride, sold a bill of goods, by the clever engineers of a social movement that seeks the endorsement of the church in order to shut the mouths of conscientious souls who prefer to keep silent in an evil time rather than dissent from the establishment and be called reactionaries against so-called progress. The whole business is so skillfully manipulated that only devilish and demonic intelligence can account for it. It is a masterpiece of the great deceiver, an imitation of that true social involvement which flows naturally from true Christian dedication and love. It is the enemy sowing tares so much like the wheat that only the most discerning can detect the hoax. It is Jannes and Jambres duplicating the works of Moses (*see* 2 Timothy 3:8). It is part of a gigantic overall strategy of the prince of darkness, which will end up in Babylon and Antichrist. I am dumbfounded that some good men I know should be snared in this web. It is amazing how Ph.Ds rush in where ordinary men have common sense enough to stay out.

The evangelical wing of this movement stoutly maintains that the major emphasis must be the preaching of the Gospel and the winning of souls, but it is easy to see that some of the brethren are nervous and ill at ease in their new role. Some of them are like an old-fashioned country boy come to town, awkwardly trying to get in step with the mood of the metropolis. The insistence on evangelism first will gradually die down as this sanctified socialism takes over. The camel's head enters the tent cautiously, but all timidity vanishes when the whole camel gets inside.

Back of all this lies a misunderstanding of the purpose and program of God in this age. It concerns first *the meaning of the church*. The church is the assembly of the *called-out ones*. God is taking out a people for His name; He is not out to save civilization or Christianize this culture. Society ought to be evangelized, but it will never be Christianized. Most of the world is under Communism. America is pagan and we are farther than ever from world conversion to Christianity. It would be necessary to have a sufficient majority of dedicated Christians in government, industry, business, science, education, and every other area to control the culture and structure of this age. We are farther from that than ever. We had better get back to our main business, as a persecuted minority in a pagan world, calling out a remnant, an assembly of the *anyones* who will hear our Lord's voice in this Laodicean day. To be sure, the church needs to get out into the world as our Lord directed, but when the Jerusalem church members were scattered by persecution, they did not go out to demonstrate for social revolution; they went everywhere, *preaching the Word.*

The meaning of the church is that Christians are God's *called-out ones. The mission of the church* is to preach the Gospel, to make, baptize, and teach disciples. *The message of the church* is the Gospel that Christ died for our sins and rose for our justification. *The ministry of the church* is to observe all things He commanded, and the commandments are summed up in believing on Jesus Christ and loving one another (*see* 1 John 3:23). Loving others covers all Christian social action. It is not enough to build better hog pens in the far country; our main business is to get the prodigal home to God. When a man has a new heart, he is well on the way to a new house and a new job.

The major issue is not even evangelism or missions; the top item on the agenda is repentance and revival in the church. Lately we have been called to repentance but only with regard to certain selected sins such as hatred and racial prejudice. Certainly hatred and prejudice should be confessed and cleansed from our hearts, but I can think of scores of other sins in the church of which little is being said. Our first duty is not to evangelize or engage in social action but to be *spiritually ready* to do such things. Our Lord said, "Go ye" but He also said, "Tarry ye."

It is a skillful maneuver of Satan to lead us into majoring on secondary matters to the neglect of major concerns. Our Lord's last word to the church was not the Great Commission but *repent.* Satan's cleverest strategy is in the church's unholy alliances with this world in the name of good causes and commendable objectives. It is the old trick of a wicked Ahab inveigling a righteous

Jehoshaphat into an expedition against Ramoth-gilead.
There was Scripture for that venture; four hundred
prophets urged them on: "And the messenger that was
gone to call Micaiah spake unto him, saying, Behold
now, the words of the prophets declare good unto the
king with one mouth: let thy word, I pray thee, be like
the word of one of them, and speak that which is good"
(1 Kings 22:13). In other words, "The clergy have en-
dorsed this venture. Don't be the lone dissenter but
make it unanimous." Today Ahab seeks the endorsement
of the clergy for the projects of the ungodly and any
Micaiah, who dares to be Prophet Four-hundred-and-
one, is sentenced to a diet of bread and water. All this is a
classic illustration of what is going on before our eyes. It
ended in tragedy and Jehu the prophet said to
Jehoshaphat, after it was all over, something that ought
to be spelled out in box-car letters to modern churchmen hooked into Ramoth-gilead expeditions of social
reform: *Shouldest thou help the ungodly, and love them
that hate the Lord?* (*See* 2 Chronicles 19:2.) Teaming up
with radicals, politicians, social reformers, and Communists to build a better world is not the Great Commission. The church has better business than teaming up
with Ahab.

10   Isaiah's Decision

"Here Am I; Send Me"

In the year that King Uzziah died Isaiah saw *also* the Lord. The death of King Uzziah was a national calamity. He had been a good king. He had sought the Lord, and the Lord had prospered him. He had defeated the enemies of Judah, improved living conditions, and built up national defense. We read in 2 Chronicles 26:16, "But when he was strong, his heart was lifted up to his destruction . . . ." Paul was strong when he was weak, but Uzziah was weak when he was strong! Because he usurped the office of priest and tried to offer incense in the temple, God struck him with leprosy, and he died in disgrace. (*See* 2 Chronicles 26:14–23.) Everybody was overwhelmed. People were saying, "If a good man like King Uzziah should end up like that, what hope is there for the rest of us?" Isaiah, the noble patrician prophet, was stunned, but for him there was something extra—he saw *also* the Lord. It was that *also*, that *plus* that made the difference. Everybody else saw the disaster, the disillusionment, and the despair that gripped the country. Isaiah saw that but, in addition, he saw *also* the Lord.

One thinks of Jeremiah's long lament over the state of the nation (*see* Lamentations 5:1–18). He paints the darkest pictures but ends up declaring in verse 19, "Thou, O Lord, remainest for ever; thy throne from gen-

eration to generation." Jeremiah had a *plus*, he saw *also*
the Lord. Micah moaned that the good and the upright
were gone and the crooks had taken over and that one
could not trust a friend or guide or even his wife! But
immediately out of all this wretched state of affairs
comes a holy resolve: "Therefore I will look unto the
Lord; I will wait for the God of my salvation: my God
will hear me" (Micah 7:7). Micah saw *also* the Lord. In a
day of minuses he came out with a plus!

It is gloriously summed up in the New Testament:
"We see not yet all things put under Him *but we see
Jesus*" (*see* Hebrews 2:8, 9). [Italics, mine.] Over against
all the minuses stands one eternal plus. Isaiah and
Jeremiah did not paint a picture unrealistically drab.
Everything they said then can be said now. America is a
land of plenty but also a land of poverty; we gain the
world and lose our souls. King Uzziah was a leper. We
started out like he did, but now that we are strong, our
hearts are lifted up to our destruction. We have become
our own priests, and we are stricken with moral and
spiritual leprosy. Blessed is the man who amidst all
these minuses can come out with a plus and see *also* the
Lord!

With Isaiah *crisis* brought *confrontation*. He was not
galloping from Dan to Beersheba when he saw the Lord.
He was in the temple, the place of prayer, of meditation,
of worship. Contemplation is a lost art today even in the
ministry. Isaiah was already a prophet, mind you. He
was in full-time service, pronouncing woes in all directions before he got around to *woe is me!* He was not the
only man who met God in a new way when he was already a devoted servant of the Most High. Joshua did it.
Job did it. John did it. My life was greatly blessed by the
book *Deeper Experiences of Famous Christians*, com-
piled by James Gilchrist Lawson. Most of these Chris-

tians were already doing well by ordinary standards. The average preacher would be glad to settle for what they already had before their new experiences. There is always the great danger of trafficking in unfelt truth—working in the bakery until we lose our taste for the bread. Old Richard Baxter wrote, "Many a tailor goes in rags who maketh costly garments for others and many a cook scarcely licks his fingers when he hath dressed for others the most costly dishes." It took a national disaster to stun Isaiah into silence, and the Uzziahs in us may have to die before some of us see also the Lord. It may take the minus to bring out the plus!

With Isaiah *confrontation* was followed by *conviction:* "Woe is me!" Too often we try to persuade men and women to say here am I when they have not first been brought to say woe is me! Job said, "I have heard of thee by the hearing of the ear: but now mine eye seeth thee. Wherefore I abhor myself, and repent in dust and ashes" (Job 42:5, 6). F. B. Meyer was visiting in a Scottish home. It was wash day, and the clothes were on the line. It began to snow, and soon the clothes did not look so white against the background of the snow. When Meyer remarked about it, the old Scottish landlady cried, "Mon, what can stand against God Almighty's white!" When Isaiah saw the Lord in His holiness, he saw himself in his sinfulness and the people in their wickedness. A sense of God brought a sense of sin. We never realize how unclean we are as persons, or as a people, until we have seen the Lord. So Isaiah's vision brought *confession:* "I am a man of unclean lips, and I dwell in the midst of a people of unclean lips" (*see* Isaiah 6:5). There is a growing tendency these days to excuse the evils of this generation, to gloss over its rottenness, to minimize its corruption, to spread cold cream on the cancers of iniquity, and to dust off sin with a powder puff. Isaiah was under no illusions about his generation; he called them rulers of Sodom and people of Gomorrah. He declared God's scorn of their religious ritual without reality, His hatred of meaningless, formalistic worship.

This does not mean that one has to be an Elijah, under a juniper, lamenting that all the good people are gone except him and he's not feeling so well himself (*see* 1 Kings 19:4). God has His seven thousand who have not bowed the knee to Baal. Isaiah himself called them God's remnant. There is no use beating around the bush; we do live among a people of unclean lips and impure hearts. The carcass awaits the vultures. At the rate America is deteriorating, we shall eventually have to change our national emblem from an eagle to a buzzard. I do not say that civilization is headed for the dogs—out of respect for dogs! These days people are doing things beneath the dignity of the beasts of the field. Read the magazines, look at television, sit on a jet waiting to be fed after all the potential alcoholics have been served. Considering the nudity, the pornography, the homosexuality, the drug traffic, the anarchy, the demonized criminals and lenient courts, the breakdown in home and marriage, the desecration of the Lord's Day, the immodesty in dress and behavior, the vulgarity, the obscenity, and the blasphemy, one feels like crying out, "Do you intend to eat supper with that mouth?" Words outlawed a few years ago now appear in bold type, and no eyebrows are lifted. Anyone who can see all this without inner and outer protest has not had a vision of a Holy God lately.

Isaiah's *confession* brought *cleansing*. His lips were touched by a coal from the altar. Why is so much said here about lips? Isaiah confessed to unclean lips; the nation was a people of unclean lips; the angel touched his lips with the coal from the altar. Why does it not read "heart" instead of "lips"? Because out of the abundance of the heart the mouth speaketh. (*See* Matthew 12:34.) The Bible has much to say about our mouths, our lips, our tongues. Our speech betrays us; what is down in the well comes up in the bucket. The old country doctor of my boyhood days always began his examination by saying, "Let me see your tongue." It is a good way to start the examination of anybody. "Whoso keepeth his mouth and his tongue keepeth his soul from troubles" (Proverbs 21:23). "For he that will love life, and see good days, let him refrain his tongue from evil, and his lips that they speak no guile" (1 Peter 3:10). James devotes the entire sixth chapter to the tongue. Isaiah's lips had to be touched with fire so that he could be God's spokesman.

Such an experience is not pleasant. There is nothing relaxing, ecstatic, or delightful about it. When God operates, He does not use an anesthetic. We do not become saints in our sleep; the deeper Christian life is not a tranquilizer. Ours is a serious vocation, not a sanctified vacation.

We need to have our lips touched with fire for two reasons. We say so much that we should not say; gossiping, backbiting, reviling, whisperings, all are the fruit of unsanctified lips. On the other hand, we are not saying so many things that we should be saying. We keep silent in an evil time. It is a day of good tidings and we hold our peace. We fear to own His cause and blush to speak His name. We are His witnesses, but too often we are like Arctic rivers, frozen at the mouth. Christianity has lost its voice; it needs to have the string of its tongue loosened. We need to take voice lessons!

The Christian experience is vocal and articulate. *Repentance* is vocal: "Take with you words, and turn to the

Lord: say unto him, Take away all iniquity, and receive us graciously: so will we render the calves of our lips" (Hosea 14:2). *Faith* is vocal: "That if thou shalt confess with thy mouth the Lord Jesus, and shalt believe in thine heart that God hath raised him from the dead, thou shalt be saved. For with the heart man believeth unto righteousness; and with the mouth confession is made unto salvation" (Romans 10:9, 10). *Praise* is vocal: "By him therefore let us offer the sacrifice of praise to God continually, that is, the fruit of our lips giving thanks to his name" (Hebrews 13:15). *Testimony* is vocal: "Let the redeemed of the Lord say so . . ." (Psalms 107:2). If we have been saying what we should not say or have not been saying what we should say, we have voice trouble; back of voice trouble is heart trouble, for out of the abundance of the heart the mouth speaketh. The only way to vital, vocal, victorious faith is by confession and cleansing. The lips must be touched by fire from the altar.

After Isaiah's *cleansing* came the *call*, a double-barreled call of divine sovereignty and human responsibility: "Whom shall I send, and who will go for us?" Then came *consent*, "Here am I, send me." And finally the *commission:* "Go . . . ." (*See* Isaiah 6:8, 9.) The *call* and the *commission* did not come until after the *confession* and *cleansing*. The go followed the woe! And it began with the *crisis,* the death of King Uzziah; that brought the *confrontation,* "I saw also the Lord." There is crisis aplenty today, but we are not confronting the Lord. Jehoshaphat cried in his crisis, "We know not what to do," but he moved on to confrontation, "Our eyes are upon Thee." (*See* 2 Chronicles 20:12.) We have the minus today; we lack the plus. The only answer to our dilemma, whether in the nation, in the church, or in the individual, is a divine confrontation that brings conviction, confession, and cleansing. The year that King Uzziah died moves from tragedy to triumph if we see *also* the Lord!

Isaiah's decision, "Here am I; send me," was no run-of-the-mill choice. He did not look over several professions, as some do today, and decide to enter the ministry. His roots were deeper than that. Bishop John C. Kilgo wrote in his biography of Dr. H. C. Morrison, "He became a preacher because God called him to be a preacher. No other motive decided him. It was not an interest in human welfare, a desire to serve, a decision for 'life-service' or any of the dainty little purposes proclaimed and urged in these times upon youthful minds. God called him." Isaiah was called to preach and was told, at the same time, that his listeners would not accept his message. Paul told Timothy to preach the Word but also told him that the day would come when men would not endure sound doctrine. It takes a sturdy sort to undertake a mission with no assurance of visible success. We live in the generation of the last days; all prospective Isaiahs ought to understand what they are getting into. Such a call follows crisis, confrontation, confession, and cleansing. Without these, no candidates are eligible. This business is only for men who in the year that King Uzziah died have seen *also* the Lord.

11 Daniel's Decision

Stranger in Babylon

Old names are sometimes given to new places. O. Henry called New York Bagdad-on-the-Subway. A book about Calvin Coolidge was titled *Puritan in Babylon;* Coolidge was something of a Puritan and Washington is not unlike Babylon. The name of Babylon appears throughout the Bible. The story of Babylon from start to finish—and we have not reached the finish yet—is one of the most amazing records in the annals of mankind. It starts with Babel, where men tried to build a tower to heaven. The history of mankind is wrapped in three *Let us* passages in Genesis. God said, "Let us make man in our own image" (*see* Genesis 1:26). Man said, "Let us build us a city and a tower and let us make us a name" (*see* 11:4). Then God said, "Let us go down and confound their language" (*see* 11:7). That is history in a nutshell.

Babylon became one of the most fabulous cities of all time and the mother of pagan religion, which persists to this day. Its mystery cults, in changing variations, have permeated this world from the gods of Egypt, of Greece, and of Rome to the paganism mixed with Christianity that shows up everywhere today. Babylon is not a memory from antiquity; it is a present world order. We live in the middle of it, and the worst is yet to come. John on Patmos saw a vision of a harlot riding a scarlet-colored

beast. This represents the final Babylon, ecclesiastical
and political, the final amalgamation of collectivized
humanity into a world-church and a world-state under
Antichrist. The harlot is Satan's counterfeit of the
church, the bride of Christ. Political Babylon, man's last
civic masterpiece, is Satan's imitation of the kingdom of
God, the counterfeit of the New Jerusalem that comes
down from above. There are two cities in Revelation.
Man is building his Babylon by education, legislation,
and reformation. Even Henry Drummond said, "Any
city is the New Jerusalem if we but make it so."

> Behold the dream! It cannot be
> A false report the prophets see;
> They grasp the starry dim surmise
> Because they see with clearer eyes
> The Holy City coming down,
> A cleaner, better Everytown!
> AUTHOR UNKNOWN

The Holy City does not come down that way. Babylon
comes up from below; the New Jerusalem comes down
from above. God works from above whether in the new
birth, in the Holy Spirit, in the heavenly wisdom, or in
the New Jerusalem. Right now we are living in Babylon,
the last chapter of the drama that started at Babel and
will culminate in the 666 which Dr. Torrance calls "the
number of so-called Christian civilization without Jesus
Christ, the number of every attempt to organize the
world in a form that appears marvelously Christian, but
is in reality anti-Christian." We see this going on before
our eyes as men try to superimpose a counterfeit kingdom of heaven on an unregenerate society. Christians
are strangers in Babylon, aliens and exiles; they have no
part in it. We are bidden, "Come out of her that ye be not

partakers of her sins and that ye receive not of her plagues" (*see* Revelation 18:4).

C. H. Spurgeon said: "I am a foreigner even in England and as such I mean to act. We are simply passing through this world and should bless it in our transit but never yoke ourselves to its affairs." Matthew Henry said, "This world is our passage but not our portion." One thinks of old Bud Robinson, the Holiness preacher, who was shown the sights of New York by some of his friends. That night as he prayed he said, "Thank You, Lord, for letting me see New York. And most of all I thank You that I didn't see anything that I wanted!" Blessed is the man who can remain as unaffected as that by Babylon!

The early Christians were strangers in Babylon. Today, because we have become citizens of Babylon, accepting its standards, joining its societies, promoting its programs, we are not moving the world. Dr. Roy Smith says the early Christians "never seemed to worry about whether they were making a good impression on the newspapers, the Chambers of Commerce, the labor federations, the universities, or the secret service of the Roman government." All that has changed today; even in evangelical circles, the new angle is to get chummy with Sodom, play up to Rome, and hobnob with Babylon. Slumping church statistics show that this policy is not working at all, but the new school seems determined to go ahead with it anyway.

I belong to no secret society down here, but I am a member of one that my Lord started after the resurrection, when He made Himself known only to His own. I belong to no civic club down here; I have joined the civic club of the New Jerusalem, the city that hath foundations, whose Builder and Maker is God.

Daniel was a prophet of God, who lived in Babylon a long time ago and who set a standard for all time. Modern prophets with their new techniques do not sound like Daniel. If one is to be popular in Babylon today, he must learn how to talk out of both sides of his mouth, work both sides of the street, and become an expert in the art of almost but not quite saying something. Of course John the Baptist told King Herod off, but he was not current in communications, dialogue, and public relations! Modern prophets are more likely to be guests in Herod's palace than prisoners in Herod's jail. Certainly no one would think of calling Herod a fox as our Lord did.

How should one conduct himself in Babylon today? How did Daniel do it? Babylon tried to make a Chaldean out of this Hebrew but was not able to make Daniel over. The Babylonians changed his name from *Daniel* with *El*, "God," in it, to *Belteshazzar* with *Bel* in it, but it did not stick. Daniel faced three tests. First, there was *the table of Nebuchadnezzar:* You are what you eat spiritually as well as physically. Nebuchadnezzar's table takes different forms today. Too many church members sit in front of late, late television, gorging themselves from Babylon's fare, and then wonder why they have no appetite for God's Word on Sunday. Jim Elliott, that promising young missionary who was martyred in Ecuador, wrote in his diary about watching television in the home of a friend. God reproved him with Psalms 119:37: "Turn away mine eyes from beholding vanity; and quicken thou me in thy way." He wrote of ". . . the decentralizing effect [of television] on the mind and affections. It quickens me in ways not of God, defeating the purpose of prayer to be quickened in ways Divine." You cannot grow a Daniel at the tables of Nebuchadnezzar. We must get back to the simple fare of God's Word. The Chaldean fare was probably connected with idolatry. Paul had something to tell us about that; the man of God must beware of food for body, for mind or for spirit, in any way identified with Babylon.

Another lesson emerges from Daniel's asceticism and vegetarianism. He was courteous about it and did not flaunt his self-denial in the faces of the pagans. That is a far cry from Pharasaism that appears unto men to fast. This world has sadness and melancholy enough without preachers looking as forlorn as the last rose of summer. If we claim to be living in Beulah Land, with its figs and pomegranates, with its milk and honey, we ought not to look as if we had been on a diet of crab apples.

Daniel's second test was at *the feast of Belshazzar* with its revelry, revelation, and retribution. America is on a drunken binge; where is there a Daniel in all this Babylon? The only man who is ready to speak for God in public life is the man who has been true to God in his personal life. The man who has said no to the fare of Nebuchadnezzar is the man who knows what to say at the feast of Belshazzar. Prophets who have gorged themselves at the tables of Babylon cannot read the handwriting on the wall of Babylon.

Utterly unaware of it mighty Babylon was but a few hours from final judgment. Recently I visited a mammoth dam and power plant, one of the engineering marvels of America. As I viewed this masterpiece of human ingenuity, I thought of a still more recent achievement in which a man stood on the moon and talked with the president of the United States. In such an age of breathtaking marvels one might say, "Surely we will soon eliminate disease, war, pollution, ignorance, poverty, hatred, and all the distempers that plague us today." But no. Civilizations rise and fall, seem almost to reach heaven with their towers of Babel and then collapse from within. All we learn from history is that we learn nothing from history. The Pyramids still bear witness to

Egypt's engineering wonders. A leading educator, William L. Poteat said: "It may be questioned whether there has been any improvement of the human stock during the present historic period. Certainly two centuries of ancient Athens produced men who, in statesmanship, in philosophy, in letters, in oratory, and in art, set standards for all subsequent time." Rome ruled the world, then perished from within and plunged humanity into a thousand years of darkness. So today men say that this time we will make it. But science does not master sin; at the height of our greatest technological progress, God writes on the wall, and another Babylon is weighed in the balances and found wanting. Men who could be Daniels are carried away by the trends and currents of the times and end up making little civic-club speeches in the halls of Belshazzar.

The wise men of Babylon could not interpret the inscription on the wall because they could not read God's handwriting. America is at Belshazzar's feast today, and God is writing on the wall. The wise men have been called in to read the meaning of these days. Daily you see economic experts, military experts, financial experts, and sociologists on television panels and symposiums. They analyze, discuss, diagnose, and prescribe; but after they have finished, you do not know any more than when they began. They cannot read the signs of the times—the Middle East crisis, for example. You see, it is God's handwriting; being a Ph.D. does not necessarily help. A country preacher may understand the times better than all the soothsayers and the smooth-tongued of Babylon.

You will observe that Daniel did not attend Belshazzar's feast; they had to send for him. God's man has no time to waste sipping ginger ale with the cocktail set at the courts of Babylon. The prophet who laughs and dines with the world in its revelry has no message when

God writes on the wall. He cannot read that handwriting, because he has not been with God long enough to learn the language!

Thank God, at the original feast of Belshazzar, the queen could say, *there is a man*, a man who knows what time it is and how to read God's handwriting. I am glad that Daniel, scared half to death, did not stand and say, "I can't read it." Today too many prophets in too many pulpits cannot decipher the heavenly hieroglyphics. Others try to cheer up the congregation by saying there is no special significance to the signs of the times. I am glad that Daniel did not read something else. They would not have known the difference. There are modern prophets who read out of God's revelation what never was in it; the average American is so ignorant of God's Word that he does not know the difference either. I am glad that Daniel did not read just part of the message. There are prophets in Babylon today who are afraid of the truth, the whole truth, and nothing but the truth. God had a man who could read it; he read it all and read it right. Daniel is not popular in some circles today. Many have been misled by those who make Daniel's fourth world-power to be Greece instead of Rome and who can see no farther than Antiochus Epiphanes. But my Lord said, "Whoso readeth [Daniel] let him understand" (*see* Matthew 24:15). Read Daniel we will and make our way through the Babylon of Revelation 17 and 18 until Babylon is no more; and then we will join the innumerable multitude in Revelation 19:6 singing, "Alleluia, for the Lord God omnipotent reigneth!" God grant us prophets who can decline the fare of Nebuchadnezzar and then stand at the feast of Belshazzar and read to this frightened generation what God is writing on the wall!

Finally, Daniel faced the test of *the Decree of Darius*. This time the issue was not his personal life or his public life but his prayer life. His adversaries ganged up on him, but he went ahead with his devotions *as he did aforetime*. The devil is in constant conspiracy against a preacher who really prays, for it has been said that what a minister is in his prayer closet is what he is, no more, no less. The man who prays like Daniel may land in a lion's den, but it is worth it. God "millennialized" the lions. Spurgeon said: "How could lions eat him when most of him was grit and backbone!" It was not Daniel who had insomnia; it was Darius who needed a sedative. He lived in a gorgeous palace, but he could not sleep. He lay on a royal bed covered with costly tapestry, but he could not sleep. He was the ruler of a mighty empire, but he could not sleep. He could speak the word and inspire multitudes to bow before him, but he could not sleep. All night long he turned and tossed. Early morning found him at the lion's den, leaning over the railing and crying with a choked-up voice, "O Daniel, is thy God able to deliver thee?" Daniel called back, "O King, you might as well have gotten your rest. Everything is under control. You've been rolling with insomnia in a palace, but I've been sleeping in a lion's den with an angel on guard!" (*See* Daniel 6:20–22.) We live in a sleepless day of sedatives and tranquilizers. "But the wicked are like the troubled sea, when it cannot rest, whose waters cast up mire and dirt" (Isaiah 57:20). We may not admit it, but this troubled generation secretly wonders whether the God we preach about is able to deliver us. It sounds fine in a Sunday sermon, but will it work in a lion's den? When trouble comes; when sickness lays us low; when we bury our dearests in lonely graves; when fondest dreams have faded; when enemies rise up like a flood; when evil days come and the years draw nigh when we say we have no pleasure in them;— *is* our God able when we reach the lion's den?

You will remember that the three Hebrew children facing the fiery furnace said that their God was able to deliver them, *but if not,* they would be faithful anyway. Into the fire they went, but King Nebuchadnezzar demanded, "What's going on there? I see a fourth in the fire!" (*see* Daniel 3:17, 18, 25.) They had company! Paul wrote: "At my first answer no man stood with me . . . . Notwithstanding the Lord stood with me . . . and I was delivered out of the mouth of the lion" (2 Timothy 4:16, 17). Paul had his lion's den too and he had company in it!

It is great to say no to the tables of Nebuchadnezzar; it is great to understand the handwriting on the wall. It is greater still to be able to answer a troubled world asking is thy God able? with a resounding yes, my God is able. He is able to keep that which I have committed unto Him against that day; able to do exceeding abundantly above all that we can ask or think; able to make all grace to abound; able to succor them that are tempted; able to save to the uttermost; able to keep us from falling; able to subdue all things unto Himself. Yes, *my God is able!*

12 The Rich Young Ruler's Decision

The Great Refusal

The Gospels tell us about three men who went away from Jesus. There was *the great betrayal:* Judas went out and it was night (*see* John 13:30). There was *the great denial:* Peter went out and wept bitterly (*see* Matthew 26:75). And there was *the great refusal:* the rich young ruler went away sorrowful for he had great possessions (*see* Matthew 19:22).

I have heard sermons and read articles about the rich young ruler and none of them have quite satisfied me. They usually leave many questions unanswered. This incident was not meant to teach everything, just as our Lord did not mean to give a whole course in theology in any one of His parables. He was dealing with one individual and one problem. He did not say the same thing to each individual or give the same answer to every problem, but there are some basic principles in this incident that each of us can apply to his own case.

This young man had some things in his favor. He did not come to oppose Jesus or to ask foolish questions. He had manners and morals and money and was one of the best prospects our Lord ever faced, if you go by our standards today. If he should try to join the average church he would be accepted and elected treasurer, with no questions asked. Our Lord seems almost severe in His attitude toward prospective disciples. One declared he would follow Jesus anywhere He went, but our Lord reminded him that foxes and birds had a place to stay while the Saviour had nowhere to lay his head. Another offered to follow the Master, but first must bury his father. Jesus said, "Let the dead bury their dead." A third wanted to become a disciple, but only after he had bidden the home folks farewell. The answer was, "No man, having put his hand to the plow, and looking back, is fit for the kingdom of God." (*See* Luke 9:57–62.) Luke tells us that great multitudes went with Him. He turned to them and gave the three *cannots* of discipleship: they must hate loved ones and their own lives, bear their crosses, forsake everything they have, else they *cannot* follow Him. John tells us that another crowd wanted to make Him King, but by the time He finished preaching, the multitude had dispersed until only the irreducible minority, the disciples, remained; He asked them, "Will ye also go away?"

He did not reduce the price of discipleship when the rich young ruler appeared. This model young man must have irked other youngsters in the neighborhood, when he was growing up. I can hear their mothers saying, "Why can't you be like that nice boy?" He wanted to know what he must do to inherit eternal life. That was wide of the mark, for we do not have to do anything to inherit; we either inherit or we do not. If we could do something to inherit eternal life, it would not be the *gift* of God.

This young man has morals and money, and now he wants to add eternal life to his possessions. What good thing can he do? It does not sound quite right. "And Jesus said unto him, Why callest thou me good? none is good, save one, that is, God" (Luke 18:19). He was not disclaiming goodness; He was saying, "If you call Me good in the sense that God is good, I accept it." Maclaren says, "Our Lord answers this young man with a coldness that startles but is meant to rouse like a dash of icy water flung in the face." What a cheap concept of goodness this youth had, as though he could achieve it himself! Our Lord directs him to the one and only Source. To be good we need not only to know what to do and how to do it, but also the power to do it; only God can give that. Our Lord tells him to keep the Commandments, because by the law is found the knowledge of sin, but this young man has not learned that lesson. He is not aware of the depths of his own heart. We are filling our churches today with people who, at best, still think enough good deeds can buy eternal life. Any man as good as this young ruler would be welcomed as a church member. What more can he do? Parents today do not think of their children as lost. "Johnny is a good boy," we are told, but so was this young man. Still he asks, "What lack I yet?" We need a fresh view of the holiness of God and the sinfulness of men that will bring self-righteous church members down the aisles crying, "What lack I yet?" It is very evident that something is lacking, and we need a confrontation with our Lord saying to us, "One thing thou lackest."

"Now when Jesus heard these things, he said unto him, Yet lackest thou one thing: sell all that thou hast, and distribute unto the poor, and thou shalt have treasure in heaven: and come, follow me." (Luke 18:22.) This does not mean that every rich man must give away his possessions. It does not mean that we get to heaven by disposing of our property. In this case, it was his money that kept the young ruler from entering the kingdom; Jesus was getting at the trouble. God will not save any man who has some other crutch to lean upon. As long as we have a few tricks up our sleeves, God will leave us to our own devices. If right eye or hand cause us to stumble, major surgery is commanded. We do not go about this matter today as Jesus did. We enlist the young ruler first, then take up his problem later, if ever. We say, "Come on and join the church and then we will discuss these secondary matters." Secondary matters are primary if they keep a man from following Jesus. Nothing is said nowadays about these hindrances. We welcome into the fellowship anybody lugging all his idols with him. People are not saved by giving up the world, but if a person's worldliness keeps him from coming to Christ, manifestly he must first renounce it. We are so anxious to increase our membership that we take all comers and say nothing about discipleship. Why did not our Lord say to the ruler, "Come along and join my company and we will discuss what to do with your money as we go along." Instead, He insisted at the very start that there must be a complete disposal, the burning of all bridges, absolute renunciation of everything.

There is a popular notion, even in evangelical circles, that we must adopt the dress, music, and language of this age in order to win its youth to Christ. We must not talk about the evils of drinking, smoking, dancing, and drugs or tell young people what they must give up to be Christians. Such an approach will drive them away, we are told, and they will turn us off. We are not to denounce sin and call to repentance, but rather to hold up Jesus as the Great Rebel and to rally revolutionaries around His banner.

Those who advocate no law but love forget that our Lord said, "If ye love me, keep my commandments" (John 14:15). Apparently some of our would-be Christian leaders have not read their New Testaments much lately. The new approach certainly finds no encouragement in what our Lord told the rich young ruler nor in our Lord's word about counting the cost (*see* Luke 14:28–33). As for the argument that they'll turn you off, the rich young ruler turned our Lord off, but I do not read that the Saviour worked out a compromise. The Athenians turned off Paul, but he did not change his message. Paul's command to Timothy to preach the Word is followed by the prediction that the time will come when the message will not be accepted (*see* 2 Timothy 4:2–4). Isaiah and Ezekiel were told that they would be turned off, but they were not to modify the message to suit the listeners. It is not our business to make the message acceptable, but to make it available—not to see that they like it, but that they get it.

What would happen in our churches if we made such demands today? It would trim off the fat from our church membership and leave a vital core of Christians who mean business. It would eliminate status seekers who write out a check for the church, but live for the devil. It would dispose of a flock of worldlings who are not about to give up the lust of the flesh, the lust of the eyes, and the pride of life. Our Lord made discipleship a hard and costly business. Salvation is free, but when a man becomes a Christian, he is not his own; he is bought with a price; he is sold out lock, stock and barrel; he belongs to Jesus Christ, bought and paid for with the blood of Calvary. There are many young rulers these days who walk too glibly down church aisles; they need to be stopped, shocked, and startled by the challenge of our Lord: "Then said Jesus unto his disciples, If any man will come after me, let him deny himself, and take up his cross, and follow me" (Matthew 16:24). He made it clear that if we come *to* Him but do not come *after* Him, we cannot be His disciples (*see* Luke 14:25, 26).

The rich young ruler went away; "And when Jesus

saw that he was very sorrowful, he said, How hardly
shall they that have riches enter into the kingdom of
God!" (Luke 18:24.) Paul says that not many wise,
mighty, and noble are called (*see* 1 Corinthians 1:26).
The wealthy, the intellectuals, the ruling class, the blue
bloods—these will not crowd heaven in great numbers.
We must love them as Jesus loved the young ruler, but
they must be told that these things do not help, but may
hinder, entrance into the kingdom of God. We bow and
scrape to these VIPs and give them choice seats, as
James reminds us in chapter 2; but they are really among
the handicapped, whose assets may actually be
liabilities. These assets certainly will not get them into
the kingdom and may keep them out.

No man with more than the rich young ruler ever came
to Jesus. No one ever went away with less. Bartimaeus
came with his blindness and went away seeing. The lep-
ers came with their loathsome disease and went away
well. The woman who touched my Lord in the crowd
came away whole. The young ruler, for all his great possessions, went away the raggedest beggar of them all.
The others were desperate but not he; he could take it or
leave it, and he left it. Holy desperation is the door to
God's greatest blessings. Those who proved Him best in
the Scriptures were at the end of everything. Today the
average joiner at church knows nothing about this. He
comes casually in his self-sufficiency and has never
heard the Saviour say, "One thing thou lackest." We dare
not disturb him with the cost of discipleship, lest we lose
a prospect. We are parties to the frightening possibility
that he may gain church membership and lose his soul.
Let us see to it that he first confronts the terms of our
Lord; then if he makes the *great refusal*, the fault is all
his own.

It is possible to miss entirely the point of this incident.

Our Lord was not assembling a band of penniless mendicants to be His disciples, as though poverty were a virtue and wealth a sin. His intent was to cut the young ruler free from all his moorings and shipwreck him on God. Most of us, for all we sing about trusting the Lord, have a crutch or two available, some resources we can fall back upon if our walk of faith does not work. We have at least one bridge unburned and pad ourselves with some earthly security, for this business of trusting God for everything leaves us with a sinking feeling. Security is the word today; we Americans must be practical, you know. God helps those who help themselves. Very few people have renounced every earthly source of help in utter dependence on God. Now if we can have these things and yet live *as though* we did not have them, well and good, but how many rich men live as though they had nothing? How many intellectuals live as though they had no true wisdom save from God? How many men of importance have the humility of low estate? Because this young ruler apparently could not live as though he had nothing, our Lord would have had him actually sell out. If we cannot live as though we had no props, we had better throw our crutches away. Whether poor in reality or poor in spirit, it comes out the same.

This is a little-traveled way and few there be that find it. They that buy must be as though they possessed not, and they that use this world as not using it to the full; the fashion of this world is passing away. Our Lord would bring us to that blessed paradox, having nothing and yet possessing all things.

We read that the young ruler went away sorrowful because he had great possessions. Actually he had nothing, for he had turned his back on Jesus Christ. Paul wrote, ". . . all things are your's; Whether Paul, or Apollos, or Cephas, or the world, or life, or death, or things present, or things to come; all are your's; And ye are Christ's; and Christ is God's" (1 Corinthians 3:22, 23). That explains the great possessions that go with having nothing. The rich young ruler refused all that when he refused Christ. Only eternity will reveal how much a man turns down when he makes *the great refusal*.

13 The Prodigal Son's Decision

"I Will Arise and Go"

The parable of the prodigal son is told so simply that it would be preposterous to build an ornate sermon outline around it. The facts are plain: the prodigal came to his father, came to the far country, came to want, came to himself, came back home. Nothing could be plainer, yet in this parable (Luke 15:11–32) is wrapped the whole problem of youthful rebellion and the answer to it: the message of sin and salvation.

The parable is the third in a series about lost things. Many times we have been told that the coin was lost, but did not know it was lost; the sheep knew it was lost, but did not know how to get home; the prodigal was lost and knew the way home. That word *lost* has almost disappeared from our spiritual vocabulary these days. Parents do not think of their children as being lost or saved. Preachers have newer and more elegant ways of saying it, but are they really saying the same thing? These days people are maladjusted, immature, maybe, or suffering from a guilt complex; however *lost* belongs to old-time, camp-meeting revival days and is as outmoded, we think, as the parlor lamp and the buggy whip. Jesus came to seek and to save the lost. He never had more poor souls to rescue than now in a generation that does not even know that it needs to be found.

The prodigal came first to his father: "And he said, A certain man had two sons: And the younger of them said to his father, Father, give me the portion of goods that falleth to me. And he divided unto them his living" (Luke 15:11, 12). Here is youthful rebellion today against both God and home. We see and hear these rebels complaining that they did not ask to be born in the first place; that the world owes them a living; that they demand right now what is coming to them. You will observe that the father gave to this young rebel the one-third part of the inheritance, due to him as the younger brother. If a man wants to make a fool of himself, God will let him do it. Health, ability, the future, body, and mind are ours to squander, to wreck, and to ruin; for God has granted to every man the power of choice as to what he shall do with the portion of goods that falleth unto him. "Rejoice, O young man, in thy youth; and let thy heart cheer thee in the days of thy youth, and walk in the ways of thine heart, and in the sight of thine eyes: *but know thou, that for all these things God will bring thee into judgment*" (Ecclesiastes 11:9). [Italics, mine.] Have your fling, but there is a price tag on it and you must foot the bill. If your heart is set on the far country, riotous living, and feeding hogs, the choice is yours; however, payday comes someday, and what a man sows he must reap.

In the second place, *the prodigal came to the far country.* The far country is not hard to find. You can enter it right where you are; you do not have to go to Las Vegas. You can even be a church member, teaching a Sunday-school class, and live in it. There have been preachers who lived in the far country, but preached in pulpits every Sunday. It is a state of the mind, of the heart and of the affections. It is rebellion against the Word and will of God. It is measured in terms of the distance between a man and the Lord. Men may drink, gamble, and be adulterers, but the population of the far country is not limited to that sort. At the same time that category is increasing in fearful proportions. Sodom, nude, vile, obscene, filthy, and corrupt, demon-possessed in psychedelic debauchery, is about to take over. *Far country* is just an old way of saying *way out*, and America is the farthest out it has ever been. I have not said that we are going to the dogs; my regard for the canine kingdom does not permit that. There are multitudes of people living below the standard of the beasts of the field. John Bunyan's *Vanity Fair* would look like a Sunday-school picnic compared to the far country today. Let me say again, however, that the far country is not confined to modern Sodom; it is measured in terms of how far from his God a man may be in heart and in mind. He may be elegant and even religious and yet be a prodigal. Remember that this young prodigal had an older brother at home, who was at heart just as far from where he should have been as his wandering brother.

In the third place, *the prodigal son came to want.* "And when he had spent all, there arose a mighty famine in that land; and he began to be in want" (Luke 15:14). The far country looks like Paradise to the young rebel when he enters it with time and health and money to burn; but when the resources are gone, the poor tramp discovers that his convivial friends are gone too. We read that no man gave unto him. Where were all the buddies, the wild companions of his revelry? They always do a disappearing act when the famine sets in. The same liquor dealer that takes a man's money for the slop has no kind word or helping hand when the man has spent all. This poor boy hired himself out to feed swine. What a degradation for a Jew! The way of the transgressor is hard and humiliating. We read that the prodigal would have fed himself with the husks the swine did eat. Look around you today and you will behold millions trying to satisfy their hunger with husks fit only for hogs. Behold them draped over the bars, in the cocktail parties, watching the vileness of Sodom in their living rooms, trying to escape reality with LSD. The consumption of mental and moral hog food is at an all-time high. The hogs who were demon-possessed at Gadara committed suicide. Mankind allows what even swine would rather die than endure!

At the end of his trail of woe, *the prodigal came to himself.* It takes a man longer to come to himself than to anything else. Youth today is asking, "Who am I?" but few are willing to face what they really are: sinners separated from God. Too many sermons addressed to young people congratulate and compliment them and cater to their pride and rebellion until they are in no mood to repent. In the wave of socialism, so prevalent everywhere under church auspices, we are building better hog pens in the far country and are outfitting prodigals away from home. The prodigal was not rehabilitated until he returned to the father's house; but the new program puts a new robe over an unconverted heart and new shoes on feet still turned away from God. Feasts are spread to imitate what the derelict enjoyed in the world, except now a minister may ask a blessing over it.

This prodigal saw himself as a sinner and resolved to say when he got home, *I have sinned against heaven and in thy sight.* We hear everything else but that today. Our trouble is still sin; we are still sinners. Christ came to save sinners, and they are the only people He does save. That is the only ground on which He meets us; we are without one plea but that His blood was shed for us and that He invites us—His blood and His bidding. Until a prodigal comes to himself, sees himself as God sees him, just a sinner, there is no possibility of reconciliation.

The prodigal not only said, "I will arise and go to my father," but he arose and came to his father. I sometimes put it this way. Two frogs sat on the edge of the water. One decided to jump. How many did that leave on the edge? If somebody says, "One," I reply, "It leaves two. I did not say one jumped; I only said he decided to jump." Decision must lead to action.

The prodigal came back home. You know the blessed details of his return: the father's greeting, the robe, the ring, the shoes, the fatted calf, the feast, and the music and dancing. Our Lord made His message joyous good news. God's grace does not set up a funeral on one hand or a frolic on the other but a feast. There is joy on earth and in heaven over repentant sinners who come home. We have lost the heavenly hilarity, the music and the dancing in our churches. Oh, there is more music and dancing than ever, but it is the music of the devil imitating the joy of the Lord. Sanctuaries, where once the Spirit of God moved, now tremble with the ear-splitting dissonance of rock-and-roll. Hippies and combos are a far cry from the Wesleyan and Welsh Revivals! It is Jannes and Jambres (*see* 2 Timothy 3:8) trying to imitate Moses, a demonic substitute for the ecstasy of sinners returning to God; but the false implies the true, and we have lost our *amen* and *hallelujah*. The only way to counteract the counterfeit and to drive out the music of hell is with a fresh outburst of the music of heaven.

It is a sad spectacle to behold churches fussing and feuding, polarized and fragmented, when we ought to be singing a song of victory to this troubled and tormented world. If we become sour and bitter about it, orthodoxy is not enough. We have not gained much by being fundamentalists if we cannot be gentlemen at the same time. If only the church could come to confession and cleansing in real revival, the music and dancing would follow.

The parable ends in what might seem like an anticlimax, with the complaining of the elder brother, but we must remember that our Lord told these three parables of lost *things* after the Pharisees had murmured about His receiving sinners and eating with them. We shall never understand the elder brother if we forget that. The elder brother typifies the Pharisee and was our Lord's answer to their accusation—and what an answer! Pharisees have not yet disappeared from the earth. Some of them are prominent in our churches. They never spent all in riotous living. They never came to want and to the hog pens of degradation. They never have come to themselves either. They sit in cold formality and frown upon any rejoicing over the prodigal's returning home. Some of them resent it when new converts, fresh from the lower brackets of society, join their church. The church members have been morally straight and religiously punctilious, but they belong to the same tribe that caused our Lord more trouble than all the publicans and sinners, who, He said, would go into the kingdom of God before them. They read the Bible, pray, go to church, tithe, lead clean moral lives, and even compass sea and land to add more to their number, but their hearts have never been broken in repentance or filled with the love of God. They despise the music and dancing of revival and evangelism. Their clean living is commendable and certainly to be preferred to riotous living, but when it comes to salvation, I had rather be a prodigal, stumbling home in penitence, than a Pharisee, who stayed at home. My Lord made it plain that heaven rejoices more over one repentant sinner than over ninety-nine just persons who need no repentance.

A little girl named Edith was made very happy when the minister read about our Saviour receiving sinners and eating with them. She thought he said, "This man receiveth sinners and *Edith* with them!" Well, He does receive Edith and Mary and Frances and Bill and Joe and even hippies. He will receive Pharisees like Saul of Tarsus if they come home as sinners just like everybody else.

Dr. Samuel Chadwick used to preach on the three sons of this parable. He said there was the prodigal, the elder brother and the Son who gave us this parable—Jesus, the Son of God. How do you relate to these three sons? Are you a prodigal in the far country? Are you an elder brother? A Pharisee grumbling while others rejoice just as the Pharisees did after our Lord cleansed the temple and little children were crying "Hosanna"? Do you know the other Son who came to reveal God's loving heart, to prepare a way back to God, to invite us to the joyous Gospel feast? If you know Him, you may be hated by Pharisees and scribes, but you will be a friend of publicans and sinners.

14 Paul's Decision

"This One Thing I Do"

The life of Paul is a string of spiritual experiences that hold great lessons for us all. I know that experience is not everything but there is too much Bible truth that never gets translated into life. Some Bible teaching is like swimming lessons on dry land. We have been taught all the things commanded of the Great Commission but not to observe them. Some know so much doctrine that an encyclopedia could not hold it, but what they know by experience could be put in a pocket notebook. We are afflicted with rocking-chair religion and shade-tree theology. We are like a man whose suitcase is covered with foreign hotel labels but who has never been out of his home state.

Paul knew by experience; his first experience was a *confrontation with Christ*. On the Damascus road he met Jesus and asked, "Who art Thou, *Lord?*" and "*Lord,* what wilt Thou have me to do?" *Lord* came last in the first question and first in the second question. After we meet the Lord, He should always come first. Paul knew whose he was and whom he served. He did not ask, "Lord, *why?*" Some of us are good at that! It was said that Thomas Chalmers had an original experience of Jesus Christ. Some know only a mosaic of other people's experiences, a second-hand, by proxy, canned-goods knowledge. That was not the case with Paul; his companions heard a voice, stood speechless, and were afraid. They were there when something happened to Paul but it did not happen to them. Some people never get any closer than the vicinity of a miracle. Paul met Jesus personally; make sure *you* have made contact with Christ. You will remember that the sick woman *touched* Jesus in the crowd while others *thronged* around Him. We can throng around Him and never touch Him. "As many as *touched* Him were made perfectly whole" (*see* Mark 6:56). [Italics, mine.]

It is assumed that if one does not know the Lord, he can do nothing in the ministry, but that is incorrect. One may prophesy, cast out demons, do wonderful works, and still hear Him say at the last day, "I never knew you: depart from me, ye that work iniquity" (*see* Matthew 7:23). It is amazing what a remarkable preacher one may be and still be a worker of iniquity.

Paul also had a *crisis with the Spirit.* I know that he was indwelt by the Spirit on the day of his conversion and filled with the Spirit when Ananias visited him, but chapter 8 of Romans tells us of a defeated Paul who found deliverance through the power of the Spirit. Whether filling for power in service or empowering for victorious living, experiences abound by which men of God, already saved, came to a crisis and found their way out of the wilderness into the Promised Land. They could have had it all at conversion, but they did not. The work of the Holy Spirit has been neglected in favor of other subjects. Some people have been scared away by fanatics; some have been so afraid of getting out on a limb that they have never gotten up the tree; others would rather miss a blessing than give up a prejudice.

Some men, better than we will ever be, have dated their
effective ministry from a crisis when they came out of
brokenness into blessedness by letting the Holy Spirit
Resident become the Holy Spirit President in their lives.

I do not know where Paul had his critical experience.
Was it in lonely Arabia where, as Alexander Whyte said,
he went with Moses and the prophets in his knapsack
and returned with Romans and Ephesians and Colossians in his heart? Nor do I know how it was with you. It
may have been as tempestuous as a cyclone or as quiet as
an autumn sunset. I do know that it is a fine day for a
Christian when he learns that Christ came not to take our
part but to take our place and when he learns there is
One called alongside to help, who makes Him real, as
we walk with the Lord in the light of His Word. What
some of us need is not the blessing but the Blesser Himself made real by the Holy Spirit until we forsake the
evil that we would not and we do the good that we would
do, so that our Lord becomes:

> A living, bright reality,
> More pleasant to faith's vision keen
> Than any outward object seen.

Paul also faced a *contention in the church*. We read
about it in Acts 15. The question of gentile circumcision
had come up, and Paul was at Jerusalem with the church
council, to settle the issue. It was a serious hour, which
could have split the church, but the Holy Spirit was in
control. I am not concerned with the details. In the life of
most Christians there comes, sooner or later, the time
when we must deal with contention in the church. There
have never been so many knotty problems as today.
Preachers lie awake nights trying to untie knots they
probably should cut. More than one finds it necessary for

his wife's health, if for no other reason, to move from one special situation to another. There is no universal rule that will cover all the problems. They must be settled on one's knees before an open Bible. There are two kinds of division. Several times there was division of the people on account of Jesus (*see* John 7:43; 9:16; 10:19). We also read, "Now I beseech you, brethren, mark them which cause divisions and offences contrary to the doctrine which ye have learned; and avoid them" (Romans 16:17). The only healthy division is the work of Christ, the Great Divider, who came not to send peace but a sword.

We must make sure that our divisions are on account of Him and not *them*—the come-outers who separate from the world but not unto God. Jesus never separated them, they separated themselves. A dozen of them in any one church can cause more trouble than all the publicans and sinners. It is difficult sometimes to decide whether to merge, emerge, or submerge. There have been times when the church has moved forward only as men and women have been willing to come to our Lord without the camp, bearing His reproach. We are exhorted to come out of Babylon that we be not partakers of her sins and that we receive not of her plagues (*see* Revelation 18:4).

Paul also has a *clash with personalities*, a run-in with Barnabas and John Mark. (*See* Acts 13:13; 15:37–39.) It was a *paroxysm* and the evangelistic team split because of it. It is interesting to know that such saints could have such a head-on collision, but we are thankful that the story had a happy ending. (*See* 2 Timothy 4:11.) Something can be said for all three parties in the controversy. Paul meant business. He had no time for quitters, but he took Mark back into fellowship and Mark made good. Mark himself had the root of the matter in him and his

last state was better than the first. He made good on a
second chance as did Jonah and Peter. Barnabas was
always the friend of the suspect. Thank God for friends
who do not give us up when we fail. Some are still in the
game because they had Barnabas. If Barnabas had taken
sides with Paul, Mark might have given up for good.
Paul was a great man, but he was not always right.
Naaman's servant was wiser than his master. After all,
Barnabas had stood by Paul when everybody else was
afraid of him.

We must be careful in our appraisal of others. A Mark,
who appears to be unreliable, may turn out to be profit-
able for the ministry. I am not capable of judging John
Marks, for even Paul failed there. To his own Master he
standeth or talleth. (*See* Romans 14:4.) And we must be
careful about personality clashes. One of the tragedies of
the ministry are the broken fellowships and wrecked
friendships strewn along the way. Every little while we
hear of godly men who cannot get along with each other.
If they do not break each other's heads, they may break
each other's hearts. But do not be too discouraged; it has
happened all along. It is never wise to put Peter and Paul
on the same committee! Augustus M. Toplady, who wrote
"Rock of Ages, Cleft for Me" thought John Wesley should
be tarred and feathered, and Rowland Hill ridiculed the
early Methodists. If we must disagree, let us give John
Mark a chance to make good. If he has failed on the first
try, give him a break; he may turn out to be one of God's
heroes of the second chance.

Then, Paul had a *conflict in the flesh*. In the same
chapter he drops from his third-heaven experience to tell
us about his thorn in the flesh. Christians have argued
about that thorn. Paul called it *the messenger of Satan*.
He gloried in infirmity, but he did not glorify his infirmity. Our Lord spoke of the crippled woman as one
whom Satan had bound. Paul spoke of being hindered

by Satan, not Providentially detained. In the world we shall have tribulation, but while we glory in it, let us not glorify it.

I do not know what Paul's thorn was: it may have been the same as yours or mine. I know that he wanted subtraction, but got addition; the thorn was not removed, but he was given more grace. Do not worry about one thorn; my Lord wore a crown of them. It is doubtful whether any saint ever got very far without one. We wonder what David Brainard might have been without his consumption, William Cowper and Alexander Cruden without their clouded minds, Spurgeon without his gout, or Fanny Crosby without her blindness. Who knows?

Whatever our grief, it can become our glory. Paul's thorn was an antidote against pride, lest he be exalted above measure. He was not delivered, but he was given enough grace to out-travel, outpreach, outwrite, and outperform any preacher of his time. The secret? My strength is made perfect in weakness. To them that have no might He increaseth strength. "When I am weak, then am I strong." (*See* 2 Corinthians 12:7–10.) We have the weakness and God has the strength; when we team up, we make an unbeatable combination. There will always be enough of all we need to do, all that God wants us to do, as long as He wants us to do it. "And God is able to make all grace abound toward you; that ye, always having all sufficiency in all things, may abound to every good work" (2 Corinthians 9:8).

Finally, Paul reached a *climax in old age*. He did not retire to a cottage overlooking the sea where he could putter around in his garden. The only stocks he knew were for his feet, and his only bonds were for his wrists. Declining years found him in jail, soon to go on trial for his life. He asked Timothy to bring him his cloak and parchments. Under proper circumstances it is not

a disgrace for a preacher to be in jail. If these times
continue, some of us may be in the apostolic succession of Paul and Bunyan, who have set us a good
precedent.

Paul was left alone except for Luke. Demas had gone
back to the world. Crescens and Titus were gone. (*See* 2
Timothy 4:10, 16.) "No man stood with me," Paul wrote,
and that reminds us that all our Lord's disciples forsook
Him and fled. Paul deserved better than all that, but life
takes strange turns. If you have the idea that good Christians are all rewarded by a peaceful old age in serene
contentment, you had better be prepared for a rude
awakening. Some saints have had more trouble in their
eighties than they ever had in their thirties. One Christian veteran has said, "The farther I go, the more I meet
with." We have been promised tribulation, pressure, in
this world and have been reminded that this world is not
our rest. It gets pretty rough sometimes. It takes a
grindstone to sharpen an axe; it cannot be done on a cake
of butter. The lives of God's people do not end in story-
book style in this world; the last chapter may be the
darkest. More than one Christian has learned that God
does not promise our reward in old age but in heaven.
He may put us to bed in the dark, but He will get us up
in the morning. Paul wrote, "Henceforth there is laid up
for me a crown of righteousness . . ." (2 Timothy 4:8).
Not now but henceforth!

One fact is crystal clear: no man stood with Paul, but
he wrote, "Notwithstanding the Lord stood with me."
(*See* 2 Timothy 4:17.) The Psalmist prayed, "Now also
when I am old and greyheaded, O God, forsake me not;
until I have shewed thy strength unto this generation,
and thy power to every one that is to come" (Psalms
71:18). Paul could have claimed that, for whoever
shewed God's strength to his generation and God's
power to every one that was to come as did Paul? He

kept his batting average good to the end of the season.

E'en down to old age all My people shall prove
My sovereign eternal, unchangeable love;
And then when hoary hairs shall their temples adorn,
Like lambs they shall still in My bosom be borne.

Through all these experiences, Paul came victoriously, and so may we. Some of these experiences you *may* have, some you *must* have. All of them can be fitted into one design. They work together for good to them that love God, to the called according to His purpose. We often omit the last part of that verse about the called according to His purpose. And what is His purpose? It follows in the next verse, that we might be "conformed to the image of His Son." (*See* Romans 8:28, 29.) We have been predestinated to become like Jesus. God did not save us to make us successful or happy, but to make us holy. Some of Paul's experiences did not contribute to success or happiness, but all of them could be made to contribute to holiness, which means Christ-likeness. Life is a puzzle if we see it from the wrong side; but if Christ-likeness is the goal, every piece can be made to fit, for by Him all things hold together.

Paul's experiences may be ours. Would that we might come through them as gloriously!

What was his secret? Forgetting the things behind and reaching forth to the things before, *this one thing I do.* (*See* Philippians 3:13, 14.) He had made a decision about *things.* In Philippians, chapter three, he tells what a proud Pharisee he once was; but now his ambition is "That I may know him, and the power of his resurrection, and the fellowship of his sufferings, being made conformable unto his death" (verse 10). Paul has moved over from *me* and *mine* to *Him* and *His*—*His* resurrection, *His* sufferings, *His* death. How many have ever made that great decision?

15 Demas's Decision

"Charmed by the World's Delight"

"For Demas hath forsaken me, having loved this present world, and is departed unto Thessalonica . . ." (2 Timothy 4:10).

The Scriptures give us thumbnail sketches of intriguing characters who appear suddenly on the scene and are gone just as suddenly, leaving us wishing we knew more about them. One thinks of Enoch and Jabez and Baruch and the three prospective disciples in the ninth chapter of Luke. And there is Demas. The story of Demas falls into four questions: who? what? why? and where?

Who was Demas? Two other references (Colossians 4:14, Philemon 24) tell us that he was an associate and fellow worker with Paul. What a distinction and what a privilege! Our model and example in all things is Christ, but among men there has risen no greater Gospel preacher than Paul. He set a standard for all subsequent time. You can measure any of Paul's contemporaries by how they compared with him, that little Jew with his bodily presence weak and his speech contemptible. None of his associates shrinks more in comparsion than Demas.

What about Demas? ". . . Demas hath forsaken me." Paul was in a Roman jail. Not a big success, he was writing his memoirs in retirement in a sunny villa by the

118

sea. Ahead of him lay martyrdom. "All men forsook me," he wrote in this same letter to Timothy that contains our text. Also, he asked for his "cloke" and books. He was not reclining in the lap of luxury. It is possible that Demas may have reasoned, "There is no future in associating with that worn-out preacher. He is at the end of his road. Christianity doesn't have a chance in the Roman Empire. I'm hitching my wagon to another star."

Some preachers are forsaking Paul today, forsaking what he stood for and the standard he raised: the Pauline theology, manner of life, and view of the future. They tell us that Jesus came simply to teach a Gospel of love, but Paul built a complicated system of doctrine, including ecclesiology, ethics, and eschatology that are out of date today. His views on the inspiration of the Scriptures, sin, blood atonement, salvation, separation from the world, Christian conduct, and the future do not fit the image of clergymen who wear mod attire, use Madison Avenue techniques, hobnob with Sodom and Gomorrah, chatter gaily in the new language of the avant-garde, and are more like the happiness boys on television than holy men of God.

So Demas is forsaking Paul. What a tragedy in these devil-possessed times when, as Phillips puts it, "We are up against the unseen power that controls this dark world, and spiritual agents from the very headquarters of evil . . ." (Ephesians 6:10). In such a time Demas is no match for demons!

Why did Demas forsake Paul? He loved this present world—this world which, if a man love, he is the enemy of God, and the love of the Father is not in him; this world which hated my Lord and will hate us; this world which knows us not, because it knew Him not; this world whose wisdom is foolishness with God; this world that our Lord died to save.

And what is this present world? One would think a definition would be easy to come by, since we are in it and love· it. Although we move in it every day from birth to death, we do not know what it is. John tells us what is in it—the lust of the flesh, the lust of the eyes, and the pride of life. It is the aggregate sum total of the setup of this age—political, social, economic—under the devil, the prince of this world. The whole world lies in the wicked one. It is the mass of unregenerated humanity. God so loved it that He gave His Son to die for it. We are to love the souls of men, but not the world-order. If we loved the world the way we should love it, we would not love it the way we should not love it.

Our Lord described the true status of the church in the world as sheep among wolves. We try to tone down that vivid contrast, but Dr. G. Campbell Morgan said, "The world hates Christian people if it sees Christ in them." It will tolerate the watered-down compromise of the church with the world found in modern Christianity, but it hates Christ and will hate us. The world means more than the pleasures and principles of the world; it means its people. Only people can hate people. That hatred may not take the same form today which it took in the Roman Empire. Modern Christians are not set on fire like candles in Caesar's Garden. More elegant methods are used. We are still sheep among wolves. As He is, so are we in this world. There is a great gulf fixed between God and man. We try to bridge it over, but it is there. Of course there are some areas where we have commerce. We live in the same neighborhood, go to the same schools, trade in the same stores. Families are often mixed. We associate with the world in certain organizations, political parties, and civic interests like the Community Chest. There are certain external bonds that bind us in a superficial unity. We bridge the gap externally in social, business, cultural, and domestic relationships; but under all that, there is a deep and basic difference, as pronounced as day and night, and there is no way under heaven to reconcile the once-born with the twice-born, the wolves with the sheep. The only way for the church to escape hatred and hostility is to secularize the church and conform to this age; but if we escape hatred and hostility that way, we only invite contempt and scorn, for the world has no respect for a compromising Christian. A sheep trying to act like a wolf is a ridiculous sight to behold.

One question remains: *Where* did Demas go? "Demas hath forsaken me and is departed unto Thessalonica." I do not know why he went there or what he did when he arrived. There was a good church in Thessalonica. It was the first Gospel broadcasting station: "For from you sounded out the word of the Lord . . ." we read in 1 Thessalonians 1:8, but I do not think Demas went there to preach. The devil always has a Thessalonica for a Demas when he is trying to escape the reproach of a Roman prison and a Pauline Christianity. If you have a king other than Caesar, Rome is a hot spot to live and preach in.

Nowadays some Demases go to Thessalonica to join the Peace Corps or sell insurance or take up tourism or do social work—anything but preach. Others start out with Christian background, but the entertainment world and big money beckon, and they forget ever having sung:

> Take my voice and let me sing
> Always, only, for my King.
> **FRANCES R. HAVERGAL**

Now that the church is being crossed with the night club and even the "Hallelujah Chorus" is syncopated,

more and more Demases are going to find Paul's Roman
jail too stuffy. Most of our church membership today has
moved from Rome to Thessalonica and from the
catacombs to the Colosseum. Demas was not the kind
martyrs are made of, and neither are we. I do not know of
anything that will thin out a church crowd faster than a
call to renounce the world. The fashionable First Church
of Thessalonica is popular because there one can be a
worshipper on Sunday and a worldling on Monday, fearing the Lord and serving one's own gods (*see* 2 Kings
17:33). Pauline Christianity is not popular. It never has
been and never will be. But the heart of the Gospel still
beats with Paul.

Demas and all his sort want their crowns now and they
will get them in Thessalonica. They have their reward.
All who follow Paul will wait for theirs till *that day*.
They have only two days on their calendar, today and
that day. The Day shall declare it. (*See* 1 Corinthians
3:13.) If we are living just for today, we will go with
Demas to Thessalonica. If we are living for *that day*, we
will stay with Paul and exchange the old rugged cross
one day for a crown.

16—Pilate's Decision

The Decision Everyone Must Make

If you have seen the original of that great painting *Christ Before Pilate,* you must have marveled at the way in which the artist makes the figure of our Lord stand out against the howling mob behind Him and the imperious Roman governor before Him. Everything else was bedlam; only Jesus was calm. He was being tried, but they were on trial. It was always like that. Once they sent officers to arrest Him, but He arrested them. "The officers answered, Never man spake like this man" (John 7:46). When His enemies came to seize Him in the Garden, He spoke, and they fell to the ground. Pilate did not know it, but he, himself, was on trial. As he confronted this strange and silent prisoner, he gave words to the greatest question of all time: "What then shall I do with Jesus which is called Christ?" (*See* Matthew 27:22.) That decision every man must make for or against. *It is impossible to do nothing about Jesus Christ.* Not to decide *for* Him is to decide against Him, but decide we must. That choice settles forever every man's destiny in time and eternity.

Pilate faced three alternatives. He asked Jesus, "Art Thou a king?" and our Lord answered, "My kingdom is not of this world. Every one that is of the truth heareth my voice." (*See* John 18:36, 37.) I think Pilate must have

123

shrugged his shoulders as he asked, "What is truth?" But let us be patient with Pilate. He had listened to Greek philosophers and Roman lawyers and Oriental jugglers, all ranting about truth. Little did he dream that standing before him was One who not only knew the truth but was the Truth. At any rate, the issue he faced was *Christ or cynicism.* We live in the age of the cynic who sees the price of everything and the value of nothing. Our hearts, homes, schools, and churches are filled with it, in a generation of animated question marks. There are no reasons for being a cynic. There are excuses, but an excuse is only the skin of a reason, stuffed with a lie. One may be a critic but never should he be a cynic. We have no reason for asking, "What is truth?" The truth has been made known. Jesus made us a fair proposition. He will prove Himself, if we take Him on His own terms. Anyone, if he will take Christ at His word, can know the truth and see what happens. He will change question marks to exclamation points if we quit asking, "What is truth?" and rest our souls on a Person instead of on a philosophy. The truth is a *whom*, not a *what*. We boast of open-mindedness, but a man needs to make up his mind about Christ. If I go around open-mouthed all the time and never shut my mouth on food, I will starve to death; if I never close my mind on the Truth as it is in Christ, I will starve my soul.

We might as well try to describe a sunset to a blind man or play music for a deaf man as to expect a natural man to know truth; he cannot. "The heart has its reasons which reason knows nothing of" (Pascal). The intellectual doubt   is really a moral coward. Too many are not willing to give the Gospel a fair trial. They are too ignorant to speak wisely bu not wise enough to speak ignorantly. A man is not a sinner becau e he is a skeptic; he is a skeptic because he is a sinner. The trouble is in his heart rather than in his head. When his sin is dealt with, his skepticism is gone.

Pilate's second alternative was *Christ or criminality.* Pilate released Barabbas instead of Christ; the world has had Barabbas ever since. If we do not choose the Christ, we choose the criminal. If we do not choose the best, we choose the beast. It is very evident that Barabbas is loose these days. The world is wallowing in anarchy with teenage gangsters leading the procession. The answer to criminality is not recreation, education, or legislation; it is Jesus Christ. If any man be in Christ he is a new creature. (*See* 2 Corinthians 5:17.) Every man is a potential criminal. Some kill their wives or mothers with a gun; others do it over the years by breaking their hearts. He that hateth his brother is a murderer. The germs of crime lie within us; the only cure is Christ.

Pilate's third alternative was *Christ or Caesar.* He was told by the howling multitude: "If thou let this man go, thou art not Caesar's friend," and later they declared, "We have no king but Caesar." (*See* John 19:12, 15.) We have had Caesar ever since, just as we have had Barabbas. We asked for it.

When I say *Caesar,* I do not mean our government. Jesus said, "Render unto Caesar the things that are Caesar's" (*see* Matthew 22:21). By Caesar, I mean the political, social, educational, and religious setup of this world today. Christians are a minority group in a pagan land. America has sold out to Caesar. We are going the way of decadent Rome. The Romans wore purple robes, and we wear dress suits; but the lust of the flesh, the lust of the eyes, and the pride of life are our gods. Whether we ride in chariots or Cadillacs makes no difference. The choice is the same one Pilate faced: Are you a friend of Christ or of Caesar? You cannot be both for whosoever will be a friend of the world is the enemy of God. There

can be no divided loyalty. A husband who is faithful to
his wife most of the time is not faithful at all. The term
worldly Christian is a contradiction. Billy Sunday said,
"You might as well talk about a heavenly devil!"

When my Lord stood before Pilate, it may have
seemed that He lost and Pilate won; but today the
Roman Empire is gone, Caesar is gone, and every church
steeple and every date on a calendar reminds us that we
still have Jesus. Let me remind you that there will be
another Roman Empire in the last days and a world
state-world church headed up by Antichrist, the last of
the Caesars. Every day brings into sharp relief the great
alternatives: friend of Christ or friend of Caesar?

Will you crown the cynic, the criminal, Caesar, or
Christ? You cannot leave Him alone. You cannot be a
disinterested spectator, an innocent bystander. You cannot wash your hands of this decision. Pilate tried that.
His wife had told him to have nothing to do with this just
man. He called for a bowl of water and washed his hands
before the multitude in a vain attempt at self-absolution.
No washbowl on earth is big enough, nor is there enough
water on earth, to remove our responsibility for what we
do about Jesus Christ. Neither Pilate's wife nor Pilate's
washbowl had the answer to his dilemma. The trouble
lay in Pilate's weakness. He had sold out to Caesar, and
when one's first loyalty is to Caesar, no washbowl holds
the answer to his guilt.

Are not these the three burning issues of today? The
cynicism and skepticism of, "What is truth?"; the lawlessness, crime and anarchy, typified in Barabbas; and
Caesar, this world-order, the spirit of this age: the problems are still basically the same. We have to live in
Rome, but we need not do as the Romans do. There were
Christians even in Caesar's household.

Jesus is standing in Pilate's hall,
Friendless, forsaken, betrayed by all.
Hearken! what meaneth the sudden call!
What will you do with Jesus?

What will you do with Jesus?
Neutral you cannot be;
Some day you will be asking,
"What will *He* do with *Me?*"

ALBERT B. SIMPSON